LeDroit Park

T0274705

LeDroit Park

A History & Guide

CANDEN SCHWANTES

THE
History
PRESS

Published by The History Press
Charleston, SC
www.historypress.com

Copyright © 2022 by Canden Schwantes
All rights reserved

Front cover, top left: Historic American Buildings Survey; *top center*: author's collection; *top right*: Scurlock Studio Records, Archives Center, National Museum of American History, Smithsonian Institution; *bottom*: author's collection.
Back cover: author's collection.

First published 2022

Manufactured in the United States

ISBN 9781467151627

Library of Congress Control Number: 2022939466

Notice: The information in this book is true and complete to the best of our knowledge. It is offered without guarantee on the part of the author or The History Press. The author and The History Press disclaim all liability in connection with the use of this book.

All rights reserved. No part of this book may be reproduced or transmitted in any form whatsoever without prior written permission from the publisher except in the case of brief quotations embodied in critical articles and reviews.

Contents

Preface 7
Acknowledgements 9

I. FROM SUBURB TO CITY 11

II. A GUIDE TO THE NEIGHBORHOOD'S HISTORY 39
1. Florida Avenue NW (Boundary Street) 41
2. Anna Julia Cooper Circle (LeDroit Circle) 57
3. T Street NW (Maple Avenue) 77
4. U Street NW (Spruce Street) 104
5. Elm Street NW 121

III. ENVIRONS 131
6. Howard University 133
7. Howardtown 136
8. M Street / Dunbar High School 138
9. Griffith Stadium 140

Afterword: LeDroit Park Today 145
Further Reading 147
Selected Bibliography 149
Index 153
About the Author 157

Preface

At the intersection of Florida Avenue NW, T Street NW and Sixth Street NW in Washington, D.C., there is an iron gate that reads "LeDroit Park 1873." It is surrounded by eastern redbuds that bloom bright purple. Each spring, residents and tourists arrive with cameras in hand to photograph the #cherryblossoms. They aren't cherry blossoms, but that is beside the point.

The historic neighborhood of LeDroit Park beyond the gate is more than its photogenic façades and springtime flora. It has been called the "Gardens of Washington, DC." Among the tulips and wisteria is one of the earliest suburbs of the nation's capital that blossomed into a community of elite Black Washington.

When I first moved to Washington, D.C., in 2011, I lived at the corner of Rhode Island Avenue NW and Second Street NW. It was the wrong corner to be technically in historic LeDroit Park, but it was close enough that I spent time wandering the streets and admiring the homes. For a decade, I slowly collected stories of who built and lived in these homes.

And every spring, when thousands of people tagged photos of the arch, I wondered, do they know these stories? Did they walk through the arch and into the neighborhood or just post their photos to Instagram and head to brunch across the street? There's nothing wrong with that; the brunch at neighborhood eateries is delicious. But there is much more to LeDroit Park.

I follow in the footsteps of Theresa Brown and Lauretta Jackson, who led the effort to save the neighborhood's history, and Eric Fidler, who documented its history and everyday happenings in his blog, *Left for LeDroit*.

I hope this book will guide anyone interested in the neighborhood to cross Sixth Street from the arch and walk through historic LeDroit Park.

Acknowledgements

This book has been a project in the making for over a decade. I've loved LeDroit Park since 2011 but focused on developing my knowledge of more commercially viable neighborhoods for a tour guide, like Georgetown. Fast-forward to 2020. I thought a worldwide pandemic with two preschoolers' home from school would be the ideal time to write a new book. I had research appointments rescheduled more than a dozen times due to library closures. I am forever grateful for everyone who digitized countless directories, congressional records, and meeting minutes from the nineteenth and twentieth centuries. The final pages of this book were made while my entire family had COVID and were written while I was a nurse, housekeeper, cook, playmate—and sick.

To my fellow working moms, especially those in LIFO, I did it!

To my kids, Mahler and Emyn, who asked me, "Can you read your book to me at bedtime?" and then changed their minds when I said there were no pictures.

To my husband, Manny, who encouraged me to do this when I regretted it. Frequently.

To my colleagues and friends at DC by Foot, who helped and inspired me in my research and answered my questions related to, "What would you like to know about LeDroit Park?"

And to you, the reader, who wanted to learn more about this historic and beautiful neighborhood. I present to you my pandemic project.

PART I

FROM SUBURB TO CITY

LeDroit Park is a neighborhood in Washington, D.C. Today, it would be considered downtown, but it was established in 1873 as a suburb to the federal city. It is a small, historic district bordered by Florida Avenue NW on the south and Georgia Avenue NW on the west. The northern and eastern boundaries fluctuated as roads changed and the neighborhood grew. For this book, we will use the original boundaries of Second Street NW to the east and Elm Street to the north. If you look at a map, you'll notice that this is a very small area. But it has a very big history.

The Early History of the Land

Before talking about individual homes, we should understand where we are and how this neighborhood developed.

Before this was LeDroit Park, and before D.C. was the nation's capital, even before there was the colony of Maryland, this was the home of the Nacotchtank. There is little left in the historic record of this American Indian tribe. It does not seem that the area that would become LeDroit Park was a Nacotchtank settlement, but this region was their home until the 1600s.

The Nacotchtank were pushed out, and the land was developed by Europeans. Early landowners owned a tract of land measuring about five hundred acres. The land stretched from present-day Dupont Circle toward the northeast and included in its uppermost corner what is now LeDroit Park. Keep in mind, everything that is now Washington, D.C., had been the British colony of Maryland.

The rectangular shape of this original tract, tilted slightly to the left, is what led to the triangular shape of LeDroit Park nearly two hundred years later. As Boundary Street sliced the upper right-hand corner of the tract, the

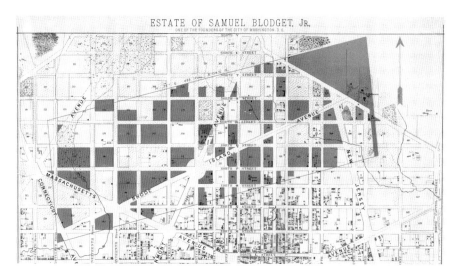

This map shows an overlay of the Jamaica Vacancy tract on top of early Washington, D.C. Note that LeDroit Park is the triangle section in the upper-right corner across Florida Avenue NW. *Library of Congress*.

remaining section north of the city boundary made a small triangle. That tract of land became LeDroit Park.

In the 1670s, John Peerce was given the large rectangular tract of land. He called it Jamaica Vacancy. Peerce sold Jamaica to John Waring, brother to a prominent Georgetown merchant. The Georgetown neighborhood of Washington, D.C., today predates D.C. and originally was a separate city in the colony of Maryland.

When this area was chosen as the site of the new capital city, land speculation began. Tracts changed hands quickly and often without any improvements made to them. Waring sold that same tract of five hundred acres to a group of businessmen led by Phillip Fendell. Fendell is remembered today by the Lee-Fendell House in Alexandria. He built that house for his family, who would later include Henry "Light-Horse Harry" Lee and Robert E. Lee.

Along with Fendell, the syndicate that purchased the Jamaica tract included Benjamin Stoddart, first secretary of the navy; Uriah Forrest, statesman of early America; and William Deakins, merchant and surveyor. These three men all lived in Georgetown at the time.

They purchased the Jamaica Vacancy in 1791 but didn't seem to have ever lived there or done anything with the land that would become LeDroit Park. Less than a year later, the group sold it to Samuel Blodgett Jr. He was a major player in the building of the nation's capital city. Blodgett served with George Washington during the Revolutionary War; was chairman of the board of commissioners that designed Washington, D.C.; and personally helped finance the building of both the U.S. Capitol and the White House.

Even before this became LeDroit Park, major players were involved in this land.

Boundary Street

By the 1850s, the larger Jamaica Vacancy tract had been subdivided.

Most of the area was open farmland or forest. A tributary of Tiber Creek ran north and south through the neighboring land around where First and Second Streets are in Bloomingdale today. The creek was shallow but still had some fish and was surrounded by briars and untended bushes.

The federal city of Washington was designed to be a grid of streets; its northernmost road was called Boundary Street. The name described its purpose. It delineated the boundary of the federal city of Washington and Washington County in the District of Columbia. Though today everything within the district is also the city of Washington, there was nearly a century of two entities—Washington city and Washington County. Boundary Street today is Florida Avenue NW.

This wide, unpaved road would have bended and curved for some of its route, but here it was a straight line that separated the county and the city. There was not much north of Boundary Steet in Washington County. In fact, there wasn't much south of it, either, in the city in the mid-nineteenth century.

In the years before LeDroit Park was established, you could stand at the corner of the Seventh Street Turnpike (what is now Georgia Avenue) and look east along Boundary Street (Florida Avenue NW) and see all the way down to Lincoln Avenue (North Capitol Street). This was nearly seven blocks away, but there were not many buildings along the road. The few houses on Boundary Street were set back in long, narrow lots.

At the corner of Seventh Street Turnpike and Boundary Street there were a few structures. In the 1860s, police officer James Johnson had a small house on the corner. The Park Hotel Restaurant was just north on the eastern side of the turnpike. Very little is written about the Park Hotel, but it appears on maps of the area from as early as the 1850s until it was sold to Howard University in 1868. In the early 1870s, butcher John Cole lived in a small brick home at this corner. His son, Bodie, was the butcher at the O Street Market downtown.

One thing you could see looking east down Boundary Street was St. Patrick's Cemetery. This was one of the oldest developments north of Boundary Street. The earliest burials began in 1808 and continued until Mount Olivet Cemetery opened farther east along the road. All remains had been reinterred in Mount Olivet by 1895. St. Patrick's Cemetery was within the land owned by the Moores. This would be just east of historic LeDroit Park between First and Second Streets NW.

This rural area with only a few homes is how the area looked as LeDroit Park was being built.

Original Boundary Street Owners

The relevant owners of what became LeDroit Park were David McClelland, Zadok D. Gilman and George Moore. There was also a large unoccupied plot owned by C. Miller.

The land north of Boundary Street around Third Street NW was owned by David McClelland, who became a LeDroit Park resident after selling part of his property. His original house stood in 1859 at what is now the corner of Rhode Island Avenue NW and Third Street NW. This is where the United Planning Office building currently stands.

Separating McClelland's property and the property of Z.D. Gilman was a straight line of oak trees that would later be incorporated into LeDroit Park. Both the McClelland and Gilman properties were mostly used for grazing, with ten acres of open land to the north. They had moderately sized houses on the tracts of land and circular driveways off Boundary Street.

Gilman lists Boundary Street at Third Street as his address in 1870, but McClelland always lists his residence elsewhere in Washington, D.C., before the area became LeDroit Park. We can assume, however, that the 1861 map showing a house on land owned by D. McClelland is accurate. The map was engraved by…David McClelland.

He was a copper-plate engraver and map publisher from about 1840 until his death in 1876. This particular map has some important history. The 1861 map of Washington, D.C., was the most accurate map of the city at the time.

Edwin Stanton, secretary of war during the American Civil War, requested to purchase the map, as it was essential to fortifying the capital city.

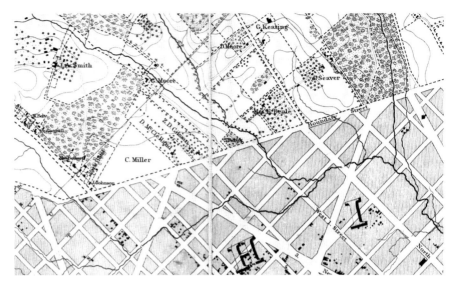

An 1861 map listing owners of land tracts that became LeDroit Park. *Library of Congress.*

McClelland offered to sell it for $20,000. Stanton offered $500. McClelland countered with $4,000 but wanted the copyright and materials to be returned to him after the war. This offer was not accepted. Instead, Stanton sent soldiers to his home to seize the items. In the end, the government paid McClelland $8,500 but never returned the maps.

McClelland was married to Mary Elizabeth, sister of the neighboring property owner, Zadok D. Gilman. Their father was Ephraim Gilman. He was a draftsman at the United States Land Office in the 1840s. He created a map at the request of President James K. Polk to show the territorial gains of the United States in that decade. Polk gave short notice to the elder Gilman to create this map. There were two errors on the map: the renaming of the Cumberland and Tennessee Rivers to the "Great Kanawha" and the "Big Sandy." These are thought to be a jest at the president, who was from Tennessee, for the short notice. There is no evidence that Mary's father's job as a draftsman and her husband's profession as an engraver were the cause of their meeting, but it is an interesting aside.

Z.D. Gilman, brother-in-law and neighbor to McClelland, operated a drugstore in the mid-nineteenth century. The Gilman Drug Store opened in 1822 on Pennsylvania Avenue NW and remained there until 1965. The store occupied the ground floor, though the whole building displayed the large "Gilman Drugs" sign. The building is most known for housing Matthew Brady's photography studio on the upper floors following the Civil War. At the time the drugstore closed in 1965, it was the oldest one in continuous operation in the United States.

Though McClelland stayed to see the development of LeDroit Park, Gilman had already left.

He had traded his parcel of land to Alexander Robey Shepherd in 1871 in exchange for another undetermined lot in Washington, D.C. Shepherd had just been appointed director of public works. It doesn't seem that he ever lived here, and the land was likely related to Shepherd's efforts regarding Tiber Creek (located five hundred yards to the east of Gilman's property). One of Shepherd's many public works legacies was turning Tiber Creek into a closed sewer. He did this all the way through downtown D.C., and it became Constitution Avenue NW.

The American Civil War

To the east of Gilman was Moore's Lane, which became Second Street NW. It was named after the owner of that tract of land, George Moore. His father had owned much of the land here and to the east and divided it among his five children in 1839. George inherited the westernmost parcel, next to the Gilmans.

Moore was a farmer and lived here with his wife, Elizabeth, and their older single daughters. To the north and west of the McClelland, Gilman and Moore tracts was a large, forested area.

At the start of the Civil War, U.S. troops from Northern states began to arrive in Washington, D.C. One of the first to this area was the First New York Cavalry, which stayed on the farmland of the Moore family. Some of the soldiers, not accustomed to outdoor living, were billeted in the Moore home.

Initially, the plan for this area was to build barracks for the cavalry, but it was quickly converted into a military hospital. Campbell Hospital was built on the unoccupied Miller tract along Boundary Street between Fifth and Sixth Streets NW. McClelland's and Gilman's homes would have been just next to the hospital. From south to north, the hospital extended from Boundary Street to around what is W Street NW today.

The first wounded soldiers arrived at the temporary hospital in December 1862. There were nine hundred beds on site in a series of long, one-story wooden barracks. These pavilion-style hospitals were common. Individual buildings would make it easier to isolate in case of fire or illness. There was

An 1871 map showing Campbell Military Hospital at the corner of Boundary and Seventh Streets, next to land owned by McClelland and Gilman. *Library of Congress.*

a garden for fresh food, water was carried in from the Potomac River and waste was distributed through the sewer system.

Campbell Hospital was unique in that in addition to a dining hall and a kitchen, it also had a theater. There is no more well-known theater lover of Civil War–era Washington, D.C., than President Abraham Lincoln. Both Abraham and Mary Todd Lincoln would visit recovering soldiers at area hospitals. Mary records a visit to Campbell Hospital in 1864.

On March 17, 1865, Campbell Hospital was having a production of *Still Waters Run Deep*. There was a rumor about town that President Lincoln would be attending. John Wilkes Booth heard this rumor and with not much more than an hour's notice gathered his conspirators to kidnap the president outside the hospital. Booth's original plan was to kidnap and

An 1864 lithograph of the grounds of Campbell Military Hospital. Florida Avenue is in the foreground, and the road on the left is likely Sixth Street NW. *Library of Congress.*

Early Freedmen's Hospital, circa 1910. This version of the hospital was built so that the facility could move from the Campbell Hospital site. This building is still used by Howard University's School of Communication. *Library of Congress.*

ransom the president for Confederate prisoners rather than assassinate him. As Booth and his conspirators waited, they saw a carriage approach. It was not Lincoln after all but possibly Salmon Chase, chief justice of the Supreme Court. Lincoln had changed his plans for the evening and instead went to an event at the National Hotel. Ironically, the National Hotel is where John Wilkes Booth was living at the time. Skipping a visit to Campbell Hospital would delay the attack on Lincoln by nearly a month, at which point kidnapping was pointless and assassination had become the plan.

Campbell Hospital would be reported as empty just two months later, in July 1865. Later that year, Freedmen's Hospital moved to the site. Freedmen's Hospital had been established in 1862 a few blocks to the west. This area was known as Camp Barker, a contraband camp for escaped enslaved persons who had come to Washington, D.C., seeking refuge. When the Freedmen's Hospital moved to the site on Boundary Street in 1865, the head of the hospital, Dr. Alexander Augusta, came with it.

Dr. Augusta was one of only eight Black officers during the American Civil War. He was, in fact, the first. He was commissioned as a major in 1863. Many of the men he worked with were white and protested being subordinate to a Black man. In response, President Lincoln placed Dr. Augusta in charge of Freedmen's Hospital. Around the same time, he was promoted to lieutenant colonel and was the highest-ranking Black officer. Lincoln invited Augusta and his assistant, Dr. Anderson Abbott, to the White House. They were among the first Black men invited to the White House, and their presence caused a stir. Abbott would later report that they could not have "created more surprise if we had been dropped down upon them through the skylight."

Dr. Augusta later left the hospital, and the hospital would leave Boundary Street by 1869. It moved to the campus of Howard University. Augusta returned, becoming the first Black professor of medicine at Howard University Medical School. Following his death in 1890, he was the first Black officer buried in Arlington National Cemetery.

Howardtown

The remains of Campbell/Freedmen's Hospital were quickly moved aside. In 1870, this tract was purchased by Howard University. The university had been purchasing land to the north, and a neighborhood developed around

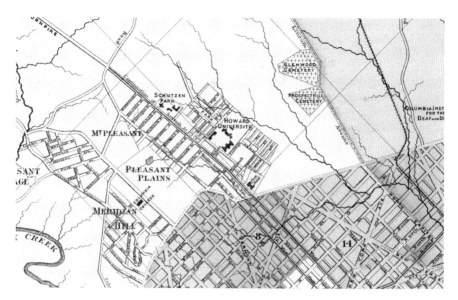

This map from 1873 shows that the streets of Howardtown were being laid. Pomeroy Street (now W Street) and Wilson Street (now V Street NW) are just north of historic LeDroit Park. *Library of Congress.*

it called Howardtown. The small wood homes that were being built would be a stark contrast to the Victorian villas of LeDroit Park. Howardtown was for the most part a community evolved from formerly enslaved persons and later faculty at Howard University.

Howard University started to lay out the streets around the university. Pomeroy Street (now W Street NW), Wilson Street (V Street NW), Fourth Street and Fifth Street were created to connect Howardtown to the city of Washington. It doesn't seem the roads were ever connected to Boundary Street (Florida Avenue NW).

Slaughterhouses, saloons and dance halls opened along the Seventh Street Turnpike as the neighborhood started to grow. Having access to the rest of downtown Washington, D.C., would prove essential.

With the growth of Howardtown and Howard University, this part of D.C. was growing into a thriving Black community.

LeDroit Park Developed

In 1872, Howard University sold the triangle tract that had been Campbell Hospital at the corner of Boundary and Seventh Streets to Amzi L.

Barber and Andrew Langdon, brothers-in-law turned real estate developers. They also purchased the old Gilman tract from Alexander R. Shepherd and brought in David McClelland and his land into the development. They rejoined the original Miller, McClelland and Gilman lots, recreating the triangle north of Boundary Street of the original Jamaica Vacancy.

Barber and Langdon decided to name the development LeDroit Park, after Langdon's father and Barber's father-in-law, Le Droict Langdon. Note the slightly different spelling. Le Droict Langdon was named to honor Major John Le Droit Baptiste du Bussey, a Frenchman who was exiled from that country during the French

Portrait of LeDroit Park developer Amzi Barber from 1895. *Author's collection.*

Revolution. He was not a direct relative but was the third husband of Andrew Langdon's great-grandmother. So, in an indirect way, LeDroit Park is named after a French aristocrat.

The vision for the neighborhood was a rural retreat within walking distance of downtown. The marketing for LeDroit Park stated:

> *Country homes with City conveniences. Only one mile and a quarter from the Post Office. The President's House and Capitol at equal distances from the Park. Four squares to the New Northern market. One to four squares from Two lines of Street-cars. Entire property handsomely ornamented and enclosed with Flemings Patent Combination Fence. Prices low. Terms easy. (Map, "1880s Plan of LeDroit Park")*

It was marketed as an exclusive option for only "the very highest type." This was never explicitly stated as meaning whites only, but it was certainly implied.

It is interesting to note that Amzi Barber had been an active abolitionist prior to becoming a real estate developer. Some of the earliest residents of LeDroit Park made declarations against slavery and commanded the U.S. Colored Troops in the American Civil War. This highlights the often-missed nuance of the nineteenth century that some people were against slavery but did not believe in the equality of races.

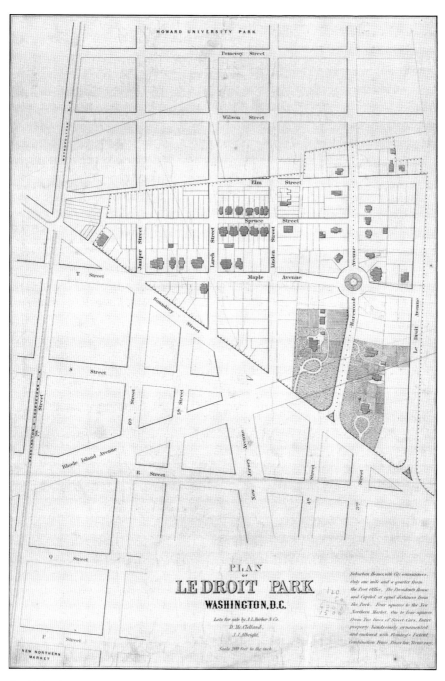

An 1880 plan of LeDroit Park. You can see some of the earliest McGill homes. *Library of Congress.*

Original McGill Homes

To create an atmosphere of refinement, the developers added sewer, water and gas lines. They graded and graveled the roads and added gutters and brick sidewalks. Their plan was to build two hundred fine homes in the neighborhood. This did not happen, but several remarkable houses were built.

During these first years of LeDroit Park, dozens of large single-family and double homes were built by architect James McGill. LeDroit Park (and the corresponding LeDroit office building downtown) are his main architectural legacy.

The first houses were built on Maple Avenue (now T Street NW), numbering eight on the north side and two on the south side. Ten houses were built on each side of Spruce Street (U Street NW), many of which still stand. Shortly after, the houses along Harewood Avenue (Third Street) and around LeDroit Circle (Anna Julia Cooper Circle) were built.

Some of the original 1870s homes designed by James McGill on the 400 block of U Street NW. *Author's collection.*

What is unique about these homes is that they were all of varying architectural styles. No two were alike in size, style or even color.

Inspired by Andrew Jackson Downing's 1850 movement, McGill built a variety of types of homes. They cost anywhere from $3,000 to $12,000 at the time, a wide range that was affordable to the "highest class" of government workers but not quite so affordable that anyone could purchase one. Between 1873 and the 1890s, McGill designed sixty-four homes in the neighborhood. More than half of these are still standing.

The first residents of LeDroit Park were government leaders, Civil War officers, several lawyers and prominent businessmen. We will share many of their stories as the original owners of the McGill homes.

By design, all of the first owners were white. To ensure this exclusivity, especially considering that the surrounding area was predominantly Black, a fence was erected. This was a point of contention for the short time it existed.

Fence Wars

Barber and Langdon aimed to create an idyllic countryside with a village atmosphere. Houses were set back from the road to create large yards to be filled with trees and flowers. The roads were slightly curved and not aligned with the street grid across Boundary Street in the federal city. Lots were not to be gated, so neighbors could wander between yards.

They spared no expense in developing the communities' amenities. Ornamental trees and bushes were added at a cost of $4,000 ($96,000 in 2022).

The most noticeable amenity was a large wrought-iron fence along Boundary Street with two gates, one at the Rhode Island Avenue NW entrance and one at the T Street NW entrance, where the archway stands today. The fence was installed in 1876 to surround the neighborhood. It was built in two sections.

The side facing the entrances and visible to passersby on Boundary Street had an ornate ironwork fence. The gate that stood at the western entrance to the park was not the same arch that exists today, though the new arch is reminiscent of the ironwork. It was proposed in 1903, but not definitively proven, that the original iron gate was forged by John McClelland. A brother of original landowner David McClelland, John owned an iron foundry in Washington, D.C.

HAREWOOD AVENUE, LE DROIT PARK.

This drawing looks south down Harewood Avenue (Third Street NW) toward the circle. *James H. McGill's architectural advisor, Printed Materials Collection, DC History Center.*

Along the back side of the triangle, the fence was an unpainted high-board wooden fence with no gates. This was the side seen from Howardtown. The purpose of this fence was to prevent the residents of Howardtown, north of LeDroit Park, from using the neighborhood to commute into downtown D.C. In an area that was mostly Black, LeDroit Park was a gated, white-only neighborhood.

It is said that a bell would ring out in the evening, informing servants and workers who didn't live in the neighborhood that it was time to leave. A night watchman was hired to patrol the neighborhood.

The fence was a prominent feature of the neighborhood, a selling point to some and fodder for local media. Not long after it was put in, it was torn down. It was then replaced and torn down again. This was repeated in a five-year-long battle that local newspapers dubbed the "Fence Wars."

The fence was disliked not only by Howardtown residents. Some LeDroit Park residents also took part in the dismantling. The section of the fence that crossed at Fourth Street was a frequent target.

In 1886, the first volley of the Fence Wars was fired. LeDroit Park issued a ban on "intruders"—specifically, Howard students who had started to sneak through the neighborhood into downtown Washington. Residents of Howardtown gathered and yelled complaints across the fence. It escalated two years later, on July 3, 1888. Some property owners in LeDroit Park who

One of the Barriers Erected During the "Fence War".

Top: A portion of the 1884 Sachse & Company map, *The national capital, Washington, D.C. Sketched from nature by Adolph Sachse,* showing LeDroit Park and the surrounding fence. *Library of Congress*.

Bottom: A relic of the Fence Wars showing the high-board fence on the northern side that separated LeDroit Park from Howardtown, from the article "How LeDroit Park Came to Be Added to the City." Washington Times, *May 13, 1903*.

also wanted to develop lots on the other side of the fence in Howardtown took it on themselves to remove the fence.

Developer Charles E. Banes led a "gang of laborers" to dismantle a section of the fence at Elm and Fourth Street NW. Banes had been a plate printer before moving into real estate. He lived in LeDroit Park at 605 U Street NW in 1888 when he helped take the fence down.

It did not stay down for long, and when the LeDroit Park Civic Association rebuilt it, they added barbed wire to the top and hired a police officer. The next three years saw much commotion regarding the fence.

In 1891, the fence was officially demolished for good. Not long after that, the streets were renamed, utilities were brought into the city grid and LeDroit Park was no longer a suburb. It was just another neighborhood in Washington, D.C., albeit one with off-kilter streets and lots of trees.

LeDroit Park Addition

In 1891, a subdivision was developed on the old Moore property east of Second Street NW. Until this time, Second Street NW was called LeDroit Avenue. If you look at a modern map of the area, the street is at an angle heading northwest, and First Street NW matches the city grid of going north–south. The block between these two streets was added by developers on November 14, 1891, and called simply "Addition to LeDroit Park."

Prior to this 1891 addition, the original Moore tract remained as farmland, bordered on the east by the LeDroit Park subdivision, on the west by the

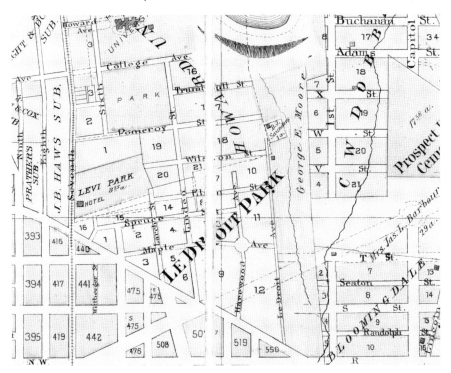

This 1891 map shows the original George Moore tract of land between LeDroit Park and Bloomingdale. It would be subdivided under the name "LeDroit Park Addition." *Library of Congress.*

new Bloomingdale subdivision and on the north by the McMillian Reservoir. George Moore's land was one of the last to be subdivided and have streets laid out. When Moore died in 1887, there was dispute over the land ownership. When it was settled and the streets were laid, the Moore house remained. Their house was at the corner of Second Street NW and Elm Street NW, just north of where the Gage School Condos stands today. Elizabeth Moore and her daughters would live here most of their lives until at least the 1920s as the neighborhood grew around them.

Street signs showing old and new names of original LeDroit Park street names. *Author's collection.*

When the LeDroit Park Addition was established, the street names were officially changed. The list below shows the original street names on the left and the new names on the right.

Boundary Street	Florida Avenue NW
Maple Avenue	T Street NW
Spruce Street	U Street NW
Elm Street	Elm Street NW*
LeDroit Avenue	Second Street NW
Harewood Avenue	Third Street NW
Larch Street	Fourth Street NW
Linden Street	Fifth Street NW
Juniper Street	Sixth Street NW
Bohrer Street	Bohrer Street NW

* *(Maps show that Elm Street lines up with the original U Street NW on the west side of Howard University. Elm was supposed to become U Street, but Spruce Street did instead.)*

LeDroit Park in the City

From the late 1880s to the early 1890s, LeDroit Park quickly lost its country feel. This was a steady and quick change created by several events, the above-stated Fence Wars being a prominent reason. Many of the lots in the neighborhood remained unsold and vacant. Rather than continuing to build large single-family homes, developers quickly bought up the land and started to build row houses. These could house more people, and they cost less. This would open the neighborhood to a more diverse population.

The atmosphere of the neighborhood changed, with fewer open yards and gardens, but the row houses did conform to the idea of being set back from the street. You'll notice that row houses in LeDroit Park do not abut the sidewalk as often as they do in the rest of the city. Regardless, there was no longer a country village feel to the neighborhood.

With the original vision lost, Barber and company decided to accept that LeDroit Park would be part of the city. But the city initially did not want the responsibility. In 1888, Barber and McClelland tried to present the deeds of the streets to the city commissioners of Washington, D.C. The commissioners returned the deeds. As the streets of LeDroit Park did not conform to the city grid, they had no interest in maintaining them, the sewers or waterlines.

This would change, and the city would eventually take control of the utilities and roads. There was a proposal to realign all LeDroit Park streets to match the city grid, but that never happened.

If you head down what is now the Ernest Everett Just Alley between Fourth and Fifth Streets NW, you'll see the old LeDroit Park Fire Station Carriage House nestled between the back gardens. It is now a private residence with the horse trough in the garden. You can still see the hayloft beam from outside. The structure first appears on city maps in 1905. Horse-drawn fire engines were used in Washington, D.C., until at least the 1920s. When the LeDroit Park neighborhood was first developed, it touted private amenities. When the neighborhood became part of the city grid, city services and utilities were brought in.

LeDroit Park Divided

One change to the roads that affected LeDroit Park was the extension of Rhode Island Avenue NW.

When LeDroit Park was first built, there was no Rhode Island Avenue past Boundary Street (Florida Avenue NW). This was original the plot of land owned by Z.D. Gilman, and it extended south all the way to Boundary Street.

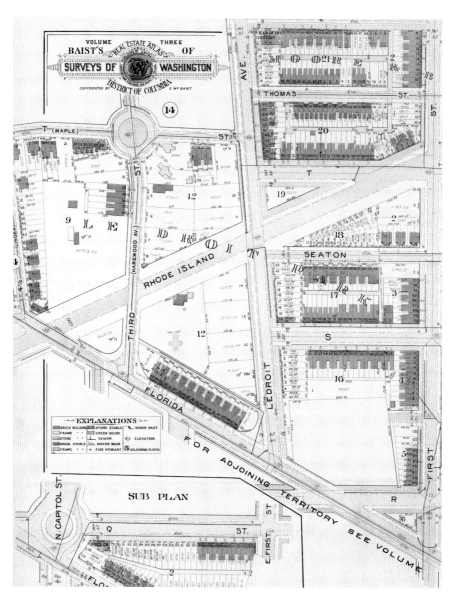

This 1903 Baist Real Estate map shows that Rhode Island Avenue NW extended beyond Florida Avenue NW. You can see the old Langdon home just south of the new road and that the row houses on the south side of Rhode Island Avenue NW, S Street NW and the north side of Florida Ave NW have not been built. *Library of Congress.*

Rhode Island Avenue NW was one of the original diagonal boulevards in Pierre L'Enfant's city plan for the new capital, but it terminated at the boundary of the city at Boundary Street. The extension of Rhode Island Avenue NW did not occur until the 1890s. While we consider Rhode Island Avenue a southern boundary of LeDroit Park today, for much of the neighborhood's early history, Rhode Island Avenue NW was not part of the neighborhood at all.

The extension of Rhode Island Avenue NW would cut through David McClelland's property south of his house. The house remained, but his front yard was significantly smaller. It then separated a triangle of land from the neighborhood, ordered on the south by Florida Avenue NW, on the east by Second Street NW and now the north by Rhode Island.

It cut through the property that had been owned by Z.D. Gilman and later by Andrew Langdon. On this property was a wood-frame structure that had been at the site since 1880. It remained but was now south of Rhode Island Avenue NW and cut off from the rest of the neighborhood. This wood structure was the Bethany Baptist Church in 1904. The congregation would later move across the street at Rhode Island Avenue NW and Second Street NW is now called the Mount Pleasant Baptist. The original wood-frame structure was demolished in the 1910s, and the area is now row houses. It is not considered part of the historic district of LeDroit Park today, but some of the homes would have been there before Rhode Island Avenue NW was extended north, when the area was part of LeDroit Park.

Georgia Avenue NW and Public Transportation

You will notice today that Seventh Street NW changes names to Georgia Avenue NW north of Florida Avenue NW. This is because Seventh Street NW originally ended at the Washington city boundary. Once it crossed Boundary Street (Florida Avenue NW), it was referred to as Seventh Street Extended, Seventh Street Pike, Rockville Turnpike or Brightwood Avenue.

The road connected downtown Washington, D.C., to the Brightwood development in the mid-nineteenth century. This is the same as the Brightwood neighborhood in Washington today, but in the 1850s, that was a distant community separated from D.C. by fields and farms.

Brightwood Avenue was originally a plank road, meaning it was paved with wooden planks. Sometimes it was known only as "the plank road." In an 1853 directory, an address is listed as only "near the Plank Road and Park Hotel," which would have been Georgia and U Street NW today.

It would eventually be the route of the Seventh Street Railway. When LeDroit Park was built in 1873, the Seventh Street Railway was horse-drawn. By 1890, the train cars used electric overhead lines.

It was changed to Georgia Avenue in 1908 at the behest of Georgia

LeDroit Park streetcar at Fourteenth and Pennsylvania on June 7, 1906. *Washington Times.*

senator Augustus Octavius Bacon. The original Georgia Avenue was in Southwest Washington, D.C., what is today Potomac Avenue. That road was so neglected that Bacon proposed renaming the more notable Brightwood Avenue as Georgia Avenue. Residents of the area disagreed, but it was changed regardless. While the western boundary of the historic district is officially Bohrer Street NW, most use Georgia Avenue as the boundary today.

The Seventh Street streetcar station was a deciding factor in the success of LeDroit Park. The developers stressed how close the stations were to the new neighborhood. Early residents could take the Seventh Street line into downtown to work at the various government buildings.

The 1920s LeDroit Park Line was a direct route from Georgia Avenue NW at W Street NW (originally Pomeroy Street) connecting the neighborhood to the Pension Building, the U.S. Patent Office, the Bureau of Engraving and Printing and the southwest wharves. This allowed the upwardly mobile Black Washingtonians with government jobs to move to the neighborhood, knowing that work was a quick and easy streetcar ride away.

The neighborhood was planned to be an enclosed suburb with a countryside feel easily accessible to downtown. This would change as the fences were torn down and the streets opened and the city of Washington expanded beyond LeDroit Park.

Georgia Avenue NW, Florida Avenue NW and Rhode Island Avenue NW all became main thoroughfares in and around the city. The side streets of LeDroit Park were open to motorists passing through from Howard University to downtown Washington, D.C.

LeDroit Park in the Twentieth Century

It did not take long for the whites-only neighborhood to become almost entirely Black.

New whites-only suburbs were built to the north and west in areas like Chevy Chase and Cleveland Park as public transportation extended farther out.

This part of northwest D.C. was home to the musicians and artists of U Street's "Black Broadway" and the working class of the Seventh Street corridor. Next to these neighborhoods, LeDroit Park became home to the intellectual elite of Black Washington in the early 1900s.

Most often it is Harlem, New York, that is associated with the cultural renaissance of Black Americans. As poet May Miller said, LeDroit Park "didn't have to have a renaissance." Many of the artists and intellectuals associated with Harlem lived first in this neighborhood, often while attending or working at Howard University or the M Street / Dunbar High School. Howard University and the M Street High School (precursor to Dunbar High School) were regarded as offering among the best, if not the best, educational opportunities for Black students in the country.

Residents of LeDroit Park included educators, activists and political leaders. Few are household names today, but that is due more to the suppression of Black history than their lack of an impact on American history. Leaders in the women's and civil rights movements worked tirelessly during the day and then socialized with poets and musicians in the evening. That same old fire engine carriage house built in the alley off Fourth Street NW was turned into a boxing ring. Local stories say that the famed "Brown Bomber," Joe Louis, sparred there once. The antique boxing bell is still on display.

As the American social experiment evolved, the neighborhood changed. Jim Crow laws were abolished, racial housing covenants were deemed unconstitutional and other areas of the city opened up to Black residents who could afford to move. And in the mid-1900s, they did move. Some families stayed; there are residents of LeDroit Park today that live in the same home as their great-grandparents. But some of the same leaders and artists who added to LeDroit Park's legacy moved to neighborhoods west along Sixteenth Street or east toward Brookland.

Like much of Washington, D.C., the mid- to late twentieth century was hard on the neighborhood. It is a time that will not be covered in the following pages but is important to note in order to understand what you're walking through today.

The neighborhood was affected by the 1968 civil unrest after the assassination of Dr. Martin Luther King Jr. The nearby corner at Seventh Street was almost destroyed. Some of the original McGill homes were abandoned and became home to squatters; others were subdivided into apartments. Drugs, crime and poverty took a toll on parts of D.C. that the city government effectively abandoned.

Howard University purchased many properties in the area with intentions to tear them down to expand the campus southward. Even through this time, there were locals who had lived here in the heyday of LeDroit Park and stayed. In 1974, LeDroit Park residents led by Theresa Brown and Lauretta Jackson fought expansion of Howard University. When they succeeded in adding the district to the National Register of Historic Places, they saved the neighborhood.

There have been preservation efforts, and many of the original McGill homes have been restored. Historic districts, their regulations and the expense of maintaining the homes to historic standards often lead to gentrification of a neighborhood. Families who lived in a neighborhood for generations are often unable to meet the new requirements of a historic district. Sometimes this was by design, in order to push out marginalized populations who lived in converted multifamily homes or joint commercial-residential buildings. Historic districts frequently required a return to single-family homes and prohibited in-home offices. LeDroit Park suffered some of this, but not to the extent of other historic districts.

The tight-knit community feel of the neighborhood in the twenty-first century harks back to the original vision of going "a neighbor-ing" in a country village with large, open yards. But today there is a diversity that was not evident in LeDroit Park's history.

Architecture in LeDroit Park

One of the unique aspects of this neighborhood is its architecture. Washington, D.C., has a not-so-well-known nickname, "Red Brick City," thanks to the number of red brick buildings. There are plenty of red brick row houses in LeDroit Park. Nestled among those are the original nineteenth-century detached and semi-detached homes.

James McGill was inspired by Andrew Jackson Downing. Downing, often noted as a landscape architect, is remembered in Washington, D.C., for his work on the National Mall, the White House and the Capitol grounds. He

Architectural features of LeDroit Park homes. These show some of the Spanish Revival gables. *Author's collection.*

wrote a book, *The Architecture of Country Houses*, in the 1850s. Rather than focus on the yards, he discussed the design of the houses.

Downing believed that "when smiling lawns and tasteful cottages begin to embellish the country, we know that order and culture are established.…It is the solitude and freedom of the family home in the country that constantly preserves the purity of the nation and invigorates its intellectual powers."

Barber and Langdon supported McGill in using the guidebook to design the original country homes of LeDroit Park. Twelve different types of architecture are represented in LeDroit Park. The advertisers of the development stressed that no two houses were alike—in style, shape, form or color. Some houses were wood, others were brick; they all had varying roof styles and outlines. One unifying feature is the number of decorative elements on the houses. These include patterned slates on the roofs, cornices, window moldings and decorative metalwork. These features were part of the "high-styled" homes popular at the time.

The belief is that this architecture was an early predecessor of the City Beautiful movement. The idea was that if one had a home and yard worth maintaining, one would do so. An increased amount of local civic pride started in one's own front yard.

What follows are a few brief notes on identifying the architecture of some of the homes in the neighborhood.

Italian Villa: These are the more modest and less decorative homes in the northern part of the neighborhood that are reminiscent of pastoral life. They are noted by arched windows that lack ornate details, symmetrical façades and finials on the roofs. The roofs are often of patterned slate tiles; many are still maintained today. You will see that the homes along the 400 block of U Street NW are mostly Italian Villa style.

Italianate: Only two of these homes remain in the neighborhood, both on T Street NW. They can be identified by the ornate brackets under the roofline.

Victorian Gothic: Only two of these structures remain in LeDroit Park. A somewhat gingerbread appearance with a steep roof, patterned tiles and a carved woodwork under the eaves make this style distinctive.

Second Empire: This style is similar in appearance to Italianate, but the mansard roof differentiates the two. Two houses have this style, one on T and one on Cooper Circle.

Queen Anne: Two detached homes in LeDroit Park are of this style. These are usually larger with a turret and a complex, asymmetrical façade. Queen Anne style can also be seen in many of the row houses along Florida Avenue NW and along Sixth Street NW. This style of row house is ornate and has projecting bays and towers.

Chateauesque Row Houses: These are always brick or stone and often feature a steep-sided roof or an oriel window. Oriel windows are bay windows on the second or third floor rather than on the ground floor.

Washington Row: This architectural style is so popular in D.C. that it is named after the city, but you won't see many of them in LeDroit Park. These less ornate row houses have no visible roof, a projecting bay and decorative brick paneling under the roofline.

The bright colors and patterned slate roof of this original McGill cottage on T Street NW show some of the distinctive details of the older homes. *Author's collection*.

Renaissance Revival: You'll only find this style along Elm Street NW. They are noted by the stone façade on the first floor and the decorative brick friezes on the higher levels.

Georgia Revival: These row houses are on the outer roads of LeDroit Park: Second Street NW, Florida Avenue NW and Elm Street NW. They have wooden porches and steep slate roofs.

Spanish Revival: These homes are also found only on Elm Street NW and Second Street NW. They have curved gables on the front roofline.

Though McGill made the houses unique and then, later, row houses filled in the gaps, there are some unifying features of the neighborhood. These elements give the streetscape a cohesive nature. Regardless of architectural style, you'll notice that houses are generally uniform on the big items: how high they are, where the entry is and how far from the sidewalk they stand. And yet they have distinctive features in their railing, trims and paint colors.

PART II

A GUIDE TO THE
NEIGHBORHOOD'S HISTORY

OUR HISTORIC EXPLORATION IS undertaken in five sections. It can be followed as a single route from start to finish or taken in any direction by segments. LeDroit Park was a tight-knit neighborhood; many figures mentioned in this book knew one another and worked and attended school together. A resident of U Street NW might be mentioned when talking about a T Street house, so following the route as written will provide a better overall understanding of LeDroit Park's history.

As the neighborhood was incorporated into the city, the street names changed. More homes were added, and then the addresses changed. For clarity and for help finding your way around the neighborhood today, this guidebook uses the modern addresses, even when the historic record used a different number and street name.

The early residents of LeDroit Park liked to move around within the neighborhood, and some figures lived in multiple homes. Some homes saw a series of influential residents. The notion of "who lived where when" is less important than understanding what this neighborhood was like at different periods in its history. For some years, it seemed that everyone who lived here worked at the United States Geological Survey and explored western peaks. In other times, most of them taught at Dunbar High School and marched together for civil rights. Officers who led the United States Colored Troops in the American Civil War lived here decades before those same soldiers were welcomed as neighbors.

Only a handful of LeDroit Park residents have names you'll likely recognize, but their contributions to American history are long lasting. In just a few square blocks, many influential Americans walked. Next door to people who changed the course of history, there were also those families who led unremarkable lives. They were not history makers; they were dressmakers. It is unlikely they would have thought that their brief story would be included in a historic guidebook more than a century later. But these are the people who make up a neighborhood, and they are included along with the notable residents of LeDroit Park.

1

Florida Avenue NW
(Boundary Street)

Boundary Street (now Florida Avenue NW) is the southern border of LeDroit Park—the long arm of the triangle plot. Most of the homes along this stretch are row houses built in the late 1880s and not part of the original vision for the neighborhood.

Undeveloped lots of land within LeDroit Park were quickly subdivided, and row houses were built when the neighborhood became part of the city of Washington in the 1890s. This was an ideal location in a sprawling city, conveniently located near many public transportation options.

623 FLORIDA AVENUE NW, FLORIDA AVENUE BAPTIST CHURCH

(Built 1962 on Site of 1888 Structure)

While this is not the original building, a church has been located at this site since 1888. The New York Avenue Presbyterian Church, still located today on New York Avenue in Northwest D.C., opened the Gurley Memorial Church at this site to serve the mostly white congregants in the area. The 1888 directory listing notes that "seats are free; school open to all Evangelical denominations."

New York Avenue Presbyterian Church was the religious home of President Abraham Lincoln, who became good friends with Reverend Gurley himself. Gurley presided over Lincoln's funeral. New York Avenue Presbyterian Church was also where LeDroit Park founder David McClelland worshiped.

He mentioned to Reverend Gurley the need for a Sunday school near the carbarns of Seventh and Boundary Streets. The Sunday school at first met on the upper level of the stables until the new memorial chapel was built. After Gurley died a few months after, it was named in his honor.

The original Gurley Memorial Church is shown on maps to be within the fences surrounding LeDroit Park. By 1912, the fences were long gone and the congregation had moved, but the church building remained.

This timing coincides with the demographic changes in the neighborhood. In 1912, twenty-two members of the Vermont Avenue Baptist Church, a historic Black congregation established in 1866, left to form their own church. Each member contributed toward the initial $2,000 down payment for the now empty Gurly Memorial Church.

The newly installed first pastor of the church, Reverend William A. Taylor, gave his first sermon in the summer of 1913. The next day, educators Nannie Burroughs and Robert Terrell (a LeDroit Park resident) came to the church to deliver short addresses to the congregation.

From then until today, the congregation has been composed of prominent members of Washington, D.C.'s Black community.

Two of its members were Romulus C. Archer, who attended church here for forty-seven years, and his wife, Louise Archer. She was an elementary school teacher in a one-room segregated school in Vienna, Virginia, outside D.C. Her tireless efforts to improve the opportunities for her students in the 1920s and '30s is honored at the Louise Archer Elementary School.

Romulus C. Archer was an architect in D.C. He learned the trade through the International Correspondence School and one year at Columbia University. He was one of the few Black architects at the U.S. Treasury Department early in his career. In 1926, he became only the second Black architect to be licensed in Washington, D.C.

His work spanned D.C. and Virginia. Most notably, he designed the Virginia University of Lynchburg, a historically Black Christian college, and dozens of churches in Washington, D.C. You will see some of his work in LeDroit Park at his home at 215 Florida Avenue NW, as well as 337 Oakdale Place, 504 Florida Avenue NW and 1908 Fifth Street NW—all built in the 1920s and '30s.

When Archer died, his funeral service was held at Florida Avenue Baptist Church, and he was buried at Arlington National Cemetery, an honor due to his military service as an engineer during World War II.

The Florida Avenue Baptist Church is still an active community church today. The church building on site today was built in 1964.

518 FLORIDA AVENUE NW, ETHICAL PHARMACY

(Built 1925)

This stretch of Florida Avenue NW had many medical professionals. Looking at what is now Shaw Tavern, one of the bays was a pharmacy for much of the twentieth century.

In 1929, pharmacists Lewis Terry and Leo Williams opened Ethical Pharmacy at 518 Florida Avenue NW. The pharmacy's name indicated that it only fulfilled prescriptions and did not sell other items. This implied a more principled business than one that sold quack medicine and had soda fountains. The sign at the pharmacy declared that it was "in keeping with the fine art of apothecary."

A Black-owned pharmacy was important to the community of Black doctors. By 1938, Ethical Pharmacy served over 167 "colored physicians" and employed 9 people.

Ethical Pharmacy storefront in 1937 on Florida Avenue NW. *Scurlock Studio Records, Archives Center, National Museum of American History, Smithsonian Institution.*

Exterior of Shaw's Tavern, previous location of Ethical Pharmacy. *Author's collection.*

Dr. Terry had fulfilled over one million prescriptions by 1953. Ethical Pharmacy was able to provide pharmaceutical services to so many because it had a delivery service. In 1938, it owned at least two cars—with the logo advertised on their sides—to drive prescriptions around Washington, D.C.

While this location was sold in the 1960s, it remained a pharmacy. A graduate of Howard University, pharmacist Floyd L. White, bought it in 1960. It remained a pharmacy until the 1990s.

Located next door to the pharmacy but still part of the larger Shaw's Tavern establishment at 520 Florida Avenue NW was the Blue Bird Cafe & Tea Room, which advertised itself as "where real Howardites eat" in the 1920s. It would become the Rainbow Market in the 1930s. The market was owned by Russian immigrant Benny Lerner until the 1960s.

Lerner had his fair share of trouble, some of it brought on by himself. He was caught altering weights to fraud his customers. He was robbed by the "Baloney Bandit" in 1949. This was a nickname for a soldier at nearby Fort Meyers who would order baloney and then raid the cash register while the clerk was fulfilling the order.

In 2011, the restaurant Shaw's Tavern opened on this block, combining the former storefronts into one establishment.

511 Florida Avenue NW, Dr. Ionia Whipper

(Built 1889)

Dr. Ionia Whipper graduated from Howard University Medical School in 1903 with a focus in obstetrics. She was one of only four women in the class and was one of just a few practicing Black female physicians in the city at the time. This was the location of her private practice.

In the first two decades of her career, Dr. Whipper was a resident at Tuskegee Institute, traveled the American South with the Children's Bureau of the U.S. Department of Labor and worked at the Maternity Ward of the nearby Freedmen's Hospital

At Freedmen's Hospital, she began an outreach program for unwed mothers. At her home/office here, she provided support for young mothers who otherwise had none through their pregnancy and infant care. This was the only place in D.C. offering maternity care to Black women. After only ten years, the venue ran out of room. With support from members of her church, Dr. Whipper raised funds to purchase a land in Northeast D.C. The Ionia R. Whipper Home continues to serve at-risk teen girls.

Her mother, author and political activist Frances Rollin Whipper, died prior to Ionia graduating and would not have visited this house. Her father, William Whipper, was a lawyer and South Carolina politician who formed the nation's first Black law firm. He had been estranged from the family in the 1880s. Ionia's brother may have visited her home here. Leigh Whipper was the first Black actor to join the Actors' Equity Association. He was on stage and screen from 1899 to 1958, most notably as Crooks in the Broadway and the motion-picture versions of *Of Mice and Men*.

In the 1970s, this was the D.C. headquarters of the Human Resources Development Group, which was directed by the AFL-CIO and funded by the Manpower Administration of the U.S. Department of Labor. Working here was Aline Neal, a union leader in D.C. who worked at the Service Employees International Union Local 82 from 1946 to 1991, the last eighteen years as its president. In 1949, she participated in the efforts to desegregate restaurants in Washington, D.C., along with LeDroit Park resident Mary Church Terrell.

463 Florida Avenue NW, John E. Washington

(Built 1891)

This was the home and office of John E. Washington, a teacher, dentist and Abraham Lincoln connoisseur.

Washington grew up not far from Ford's Theatre, where President Lincoln was assassinated, at his grandmother's boardinghouse on E Street NW. As a child, he heard stories about the Lincolns and Washington, D.C. life during the American Civil War.

His family moved farther north in D.C., and he attended M Street / Dunbar High. He was in the cadet program during school, where he was an usher at the funeral of Blanche K. Bruce. Bruce was an enslaved man who would become the first Black man to serve a full term in the U.S. Senate. He lived not far from the M Street School.

Like many of his neighbors in LeDroit Park, Washington attended Howard University. He earned a teaching degree, then he attended dental school at night. Washington was the first Black man to pass D.C.'s dental board. He purchased this home in 1908. This stretch of Florida had several medical offices. At first, he was not allowed to teach while practicing dentistry, but by 1920, he was running an off-hours dental practice, most likely out of his home here. He returned to Howard to earn a bachelor's, his third degree from the university. His wife, Virginia, returned with him to receive her bachelor's, years after first earning a pharmacy degree.

Cover of *They Knew Lincoln* by John E. Washington. *Author's collection.*

In 1935, journalist David Rankin Barber published a piece in which he claimed that Elizabeth Keckley, author of *Behind the Scenes, or Thirty Years a Slave, and Four Years in the White House*, was not a real person. Washington knew firsthand that she was associated with the Lincolns. He was determined to correct this rumor and planned to publish a pamphlet about Keckley. This turned into a book, published in 1942, *They Knew Lincoln*. It was a collection of stories of Black Washingtonians who knew and were associated with President Lincoln and that era of American history. Washington hoped his book would be "the colored side of Lincolnia." Earlier Lincoln biographers had also interviewed those who knew Lincoln, but they had always ignored the voices of the Black Americans in his life. The book was well received. Lincoln biographer Carl Sandburg wrote the introduction.

The Washingtons lived in this house for nearly five decades; its walls were filled with books, maps and photos related to Abraham Lincoln.

455 FLORIDA AVENUE NW, HARRISON'S CAFE

(Built 1893)

A few houses back, at number 467, was Robert Harrison's candy shop, which he opened in 1920 to sell his famous Harrison's Old Fashioned Molasses Kisses. Shortly after, in 1923, he opened Harrison's Cafe at this location at 455, adjacent to his home.

Harrison's Cafe on Florida Avenue. *Scurlock Studio Records, Archives Center, National Museum of American History, Smithsonian Institution.*

Robert Harrison was a native Washingtonian who learned the art of service as a butler in an Ohio congressman's house. He learned the culinary arts by traveling Europe while working for a wealthy businessman in the 1890s.

Harrison's Cafe was a staple in the community for forty years. It was advertised as "a particular place for particular people." It was included under the tavern section in the 1941 edition of "The Negro Motorist Green Book."

You could get homemade ice cream, a hamburger or a lobster dinner. The establishment had a private room upstairs where patrons could drink "all nite." The Golden Room next door was a private banquet hall.

The goal was to offer first-class dining to the local Black community, which Harrison did until his death in 1957. The café survived only a few more years before shuttering in 1962.

1822 FOURTH STREET NW, DR. CARSON'S PRIVATE HOSPITAL

(Built 1891)

Between 1918 and 1938, this was the private hospital of Dr. Simeon Carson. Dr. Carson graduated from the University of Michigan Medical School in 1903. He moved to Washington, D.C., five years later to accept a job as assistant chief of surgery at Freedmen's Hospital. At the time, Freedmen's (now Howard) Hospital was the only place in D.C. where Black physicians could attend to patients.

There was a gap in care for those who were not poor enough to be treated at Freedmen's Hospital. Dr. Carson and two colleagues formed a traveling surgery unit to tend to patients in their homes. He kept a folding operating table in his car. The trio, nicknamed the "Cripple Creek Gang," had no fatalities during their tenure.

Dr. Carson left the position at Freedmen's Hospital to open his private hospital in 1918. Until its closure in 1938, more than six thousand surgeries were performed at this location. All major operations were $150, which included two weeks of recovery at the hospital.

There were fifteen beds at this hospital. The first floor served as waiting, examination and consultation rooms. The second floor contained the operating room. Recovery rooms were on the top floor. The hospital was

CARSON'S PRIVATE HOSPITAL
WASHINGTON, D. C.

Hospital Modernly Equipped

ONLY SURGICAL AND MATERNITY CASES ACCEPTED
ALL OPERATIONS AND AFTER-CARE by SIMEON L. CARSON, M.D.
REGISTERED NURSES IN ATTENDANCE
NO TRAINING SCHOOL
Patients Accepted From Any State
Address: SIMEON L. CARSON, M.D., 1822 Fourth St., N.W., Wash., D.C.

Dr. Carson's Private Hospital advertisement. *Journal of the National Medical Association. United States, National Medical Association, 1919.*

renowned for the care and skill of Dr. Carson. At times during his career, he was the only, if not the first, Black surgeon given privileges at the nearby Garfield Hospital for white patients.

While this was his hospital, Carson lived nearby on Third Street NW, where the Slowe Hall condominiums stand today.

399 Third Street NW, Frazier's Funeral Home

(Built 1889)

This is a newly renovated six-apartment building, but it used to be a funeral home. It was built as three row houses uniquely combined on a corner lot in 1890. When mortician Thomas Frazier moved in in 1929, his family lived upstairs and operated the funeral home on the lower levels. There was a smoking lounge for men, a slumber room for family members to privately pay respects and a garage for the funeral coach.

Like other funeral homes in the area, it was a staple in the Black community. Families would often rely on one establishment through generations. When Frazier was alive, he served the professional and working-class community of LeDroit Park and neighboring areas. When the neighborhood changed, so did the businesses. Rather than working-class, day-long funeral services, there were government-funded funerals for deaths due to shootings or drugs. The funeral home outlived Thomas Frazier, whose successors fought over finances and control until it closed in 2007.

This is one of many former funeral homes that have been converted into luxury apartments.

1844 Third Street NW, Elks Lodge

(Built 1968)

Imagine a vast, open space, tree-lined walkways and a stately mansion. On this corner was the original home of LeDroit Park founder David McClelland. His ownership of the land predated LeDroit Park, but after the suburb was founded, he had James McGill design an addition to his home. The earlier part of his home can be seen on maps as far back as the 1850s. The two sections of the house are noticeable on early real estate maps; the newer half was brick, and the earlier half was wood.

McClelland lived here until his death in 1896, and his family remained for the next twenty years.

In 1903, there were still remnants of the old neighborhood's border fence on his property. The grounds of McClelland's property were exquisitely gardened. An old-fashioned garden of boxwoods, popular in the early republic, was still maintained on the grounds.

Members posed outside the Elks Home at Third Street and Rhode Island Avenue NW, formally the home of David McClelland. *DC History Center.*

The historic McClelland house was purchased by the Elks in 1925. The Improved Benevolent and Protective Order of the Elks of the World was a Black fraternal organization established in 1897. It was modeled after the Benevolent and Protective Order of Elks, an all-white organization that refused to let Black men join. The Elks Columbia Lodge number 85 was established in 1906 and purchased the old McClelland house in 1925.

The Elks were known for their parades, concerts and dances in the 1930s and '40s. This was a time when not all community spaces were open to the Black residents of Washington, D.C. The Elks welcomed neighbors to outdoor concerts and threw parades down U Street NW in the nearby Shaw neighborhood.

By the 1960s, the Elks had sold a majority of the extensive yard. It became a Safeway grocery story and is now the United Planning Organization. Nearby, you'll see a smaller building that is the home to the Order today.

237 Rhode Island Avenue NW

Before the row houses here were built in the early 1900s, this was originally part of Z.D. Gilman's land. Hewas one of the three original landowners of what became LeDroit Park.

Andrew Langdon (1874–84)

After the development of the suburb, Andrew Langdon, an original founder of LeDroit Park, had his house built here, designed by McGill in 1874. His directory listings follow the growth of LeDroit Park. In 1874, it simply stated that he lived in LeDroit Park but included no street address. The next two years, while the subdivision was being built, his address was listed as "Third and Boundary." By 1877, the address was 1801 Harewood Avenue, officially part of the subdivision.

Both before and after dabbling in real estate, Langdon's primary venture was coal. He was one of the largest individual producers of coal. This would remain his address until 1884, when the Washington, D.C. directory reported that he had moved to New York. At this point, his real estate partner, another of LeDroit Park's founders, Amzi Barber, moved to the property.

Amzi Barber (1884)

Amzi L. Barber grew up in Ohio, the son of a paster in the Congregationalist Church. He attended Oberlin College, the same university that future LeDroit Park residents Mary Church Terrell and Anna Julia Cooper would graduate from as pioneers in education as Black women. Rather than continuing in the family vocation in the church, Barber accepted a teaching position at Howard University.

Though Howard is often thought of as a historically Black university, it is important to remember that its founding leadership was mostly white. Barber taught mathematics and natural philosophy. He was also principal of the Normal and Preparatory Department. He resigned from Howard University in 1873, the same year LeDroit Park was established.

While Barber is often associated with LeDroit Park, he was also an early developer of Columbia Heights in Northwest D.C. Not long after the first homes were built in LeDroit Park, he moved to Fourteenth Street NW. Here

A GUIDE TO THE NEIGHBORHOOD'S HISTORY

he built one of the grandest mansions in the city. Belmont, as it was called, was named after his wife's hometown of Belmont, New York.

If you mention Barber's name to historically minded New Yorkers, they won't think of the Washington, D.C. suburbs. Outside of the nation's capital, Barber was "America's Asphalt King" and was responsible for paving seventy American cities. His company had provided almost 50 percent of the asphalt in the United States by 1896.

Barber was not at this LeDroit Park house for very long. He presumably lived here while construction was finishing on his Columbia Heights home

GEORGE ELDRIDGE (1885)

By 1885, the former Langdon home was the residence of George D. Eldridge, an actuary. While living in this house, he worked for National Life and Maturity Association of Washington, D.C. He would later be vice-president and actuary of Mutual Reserve Life Insurance Company of New York, which operated out of the aptly named Mutual Reserve Building at 305 Broadway in New York City. Interestingly, this building would later be renamed the Langdon Building—but it had no relation to Andrew Langdon.

FRANK BENTON (1900)

In 1900, this house was home to Frank Benton. An importer of French and Syrian bees, he was also an assistant etymologist at the U.S. Department of Agriculture, where he was the first apiculture specialist. He leaves a legacy of being the inventor of the Benton Bee cage, still used to ship queen bees. He also brought to America a species known as the "Holy Land" bees from Palestine.

Around this time at the turn of the twentieth century, Rhode Island Avenue NW was extended past Florida Avenue NW. The home remained but was now south of Rhode Island Avenue NW for a few more years before it was demolished and replaced by row houses.

53

Hilda Wilkinson Brown (1937–)

On the north side of Rhode Island Avenue NW, the homes on the corner of Second Street NW were built in 1909.

In 1937, Hilda Wilkinson and her husband, Schley Brown, purchased townhome at 237 on Rhode Island Avenue NW on the corner of LeDroit Park. From her home here, Brown painted views of Third Street, Griffith Stadium and the scene from her kitchen balcony.

Wilkinson was born in Washington, D.C., and attended M Street / Dunbar High School, Miner Normal Teacher College and Howard University. When she returned to D.C. after attending Columbia University, she taught at her alma maters. From her home here on Rhode Island Avenue NW she walked through LeDroit Park to teach at Miner Normal School and Howard.

Hilda Wilkinson Brown's *Third and Rhode Island* shows the corner near her LeDroit Park home. *Smithsonian American Art Museum, Gift of Lilian Thomas Burwell, 2011.21, © Lilian Thomas Burwell.*

Wilkinson was a forerunner in teaching art as a means of creative expression. Previously, art instruction often focused on copying other artists. She focused on a student's individual creativity.

Her work has been exhibited at the National Gallery of Art and Howard University and is on display at the Smithsonian American Art Museum.

220 Rhode Island NW, Dr. Franklin Frazier

(Built 1910)

Where these houses are now was still part of the original home of Andrew Langdon, likely around the back garden of his house.

Dr. Franklin Frazier lived in one of these row houses in the mid-1900s. He graduated from Howard University with honors and as class president. He returned to Howard after attending Clark University, the New York School of Social Work and the University of Chicago and then teaching at Morehouse College and Fisk University. He taught at Howard University from 1934 until his death in 1962.

A 1943 poster from the Office of War Information about Dr. Franklin Frazier. *Charles Henry Alston (1907–77), artist. U.S. National Archives and Records Administration.*

Dr. Frazier was a sociologist who focused on social change, race relations and the Black family. His PhD dissertation, published in 1939, "The Negro Family in the United States," was the first sociological study on the Black community written by a Black person. The study focused on historical influences on Black families from slavery until the 1930s.

213 Florida NW, Dr. Algernon Jackson

(Built 1899)

While this address wouldn't be considered LeDroit Park today, it was part of the original historic neighborhood. This row of houses along Florida Avenue NW was built before Rhode Island Avenue NW extended to cut out this corner from the neighborhood.

From at least 1919 until his death in 1942, Dr. Algernon B. Jackson lived in this house. Dr. Jackson was a prominent physician in Philadelphia before accepting a teaching position at Howard University. He was the first and only Black surgeon at the Philadelphia Polyclinic Hospital. He was the first Black fellow at the American College of Physicians and the first Black graduate of Jefferson Medical College in Philadelphia.

He founded the Mercy Hospital School for Nurses. At Howard, he taught bacteriology and public health and was director of the School of Public Health and later physician in charge at Howard University.

He was a leader in the National Negro Health movement, which sought to increase personal hygiene and public health in the Black community to lower the mortality and illness rates. He was criticized for his belief in separating the Black community between North and South. His view on personal responsibility to public health was tinged with classism in that regard. He wrote columns for newspapers in Baltimore, Pittsburgh, Chicago and New York focusing on health advice for the Black community.

2

Anna Julia Cooper Circle (LeDroit Circle)

W hile this iteration of a traffic circle dates only to the 1980s, the original plans of LeDroit Park included a circle park here. Originally called LeDroit Circle, it was a public park for the residents of the neighborhood. In the early 1900s, a streetcar ran along Third Street NW around the circle. This route of the Washington Traction and Electric Company brought public transportation into the neighborhood rather than at the Seventh Street Station outside LeDroit Park.

When the streets were opened to through traffic, Third Street NW cut through the park instead of routing around the circle. To restore the historic features of the community, the park was re-created.

Within this next block, we'll see a mix of original McGill homes, row houses that began to fill in the neighborhood in the late nineteenth century and mid-twentieth-century construction. When the neighborhood changed to working class in the mid-1900s, some of the historic homes fell into disrepair or were demolished to build urban-centric structures, like dormitories.

1859 THIRD STREET NW, BARTON W. EVERMANN

(Built 1889)

The house is one of the original LeDroit Park homes. It was built for Dr. Thomas B. Campbell. He was medical director of the Ohio Valley and later Mutual Reserve Life Insurance Companies. His colleague at Mutual Reserve, George Eldridge, lived down the street at the intersection of Third Street NW and Florida Avenue NW.

Barton Evermann moved into the house in 1895. He was a scientist and prominent member of the U.S. Bureau of Fisheries during his time in Washington, D.C. He was also curator of fish at the Smithsonian Institution. Like many LeDroit Park residents, he was involved in the public-school education system of D.C. From 1906 to 1910, he served as vice-president on the board of education.

Though he originally focused on the study of birds, he became an expert on fishes. His work as a zoologist includes over three hundred papers relating to fish, birds and other small mammals. At the urging of President Teddy Roosevelt, he went west and discovered two new species of trout.

There are four types of fish and a volcano in the Pacific Ocean named in his honor. As director of the California Academy of Sciences, Evermann led the expedition to explore an island range off the west coast of Mexico. Mount Evermann can be found there.

He lived here with his family for just a few years before moving to 412 T Street NW. His family lived in LeDroit Park for at least a decade but then moved closer to Columbia Heights by 1905. His son, the fantastically named Toxaway Bronte Evermann, accompanied his father on many expeditions and lived with him at the T Street house before attending Cornell University.

1883 Third Street NW, Joseph Nelson Rose

(Built 1883)

The house at 1883 Third Street NW was built in 1883. It was built for clothier E.B. Barnum, who first lived on the other side of LeDroit Park on U Street NW in the 1870s.

After Barnum died, Joseph Nelson Rose lived here. Rose moved to D.C. after graduating from Wabash College with a PhD in botany. He was employed at the U.S. Department of Agriculture, where he was first assistant botanist. In 1896, he was working as curator for the National Museum (what we know as the Smithsonian Institution today). Rose was an expert in cacti. He made many trips to Mexico, returning with specimens for the Smithsonian and the New York Botanical Garden.

BRITTON AND ROSE

PLATE XXXIV

M. E. Eaton del.

1. Part of joint of *Opuntia leucotricha*.   3. Joint of *Opuntia lasiacantha*.
2. Part of joint of *Opuntia maxima*.   4. Joint of *Opuntia robusta*.
(All natural size.)

Watercolor of cactus species by British artist Mary Emily Eaton for Joseph Nelson Rose's *The Cactaceae* (vol. 1, plate XXXIV). *Britton and Rose, The Cactaceae, 1919–23.*

Rose authored over two hundred works and is still considered one of the leading authorities on cacti. There are four genera of plants named after him: a gourd, two types of flowering herbs and, of course, a cactus. Surprisingly, there is also a type of catfish named in his honor.

1881 Third Street NW, Henry Gannett

(Original Demolished, Current Structure Built 1964)

The building at number 1881 is noticeably not from the 1880s, like many of the other homes in this part of the neighborhood. This apartment building was erected in 1964. In the mid-twentieth century, more multifamily homes were being built and former single-family homes being turned into apartments.

When there was an original McGill home here, this was the home to Henry Gannett. Like many other of the original suburb residents, he found

Henry Gannett's home on Harewood Avenue, now demolished. *James H. McGill's architectural advisor, Printed Materials Collection, DC History Center.*

success in a unique field, and this led to enough wealth to purchase a home here and enough clout to fit in. Gannett's work is the reason the research for this book is even possible.

Called the "Father of Mapmaking in America," Gannett lobbied for the creation of a central government agency to focus on mapping the country. The United States Geological Survey was created in 1879. Gannett oversaw mapping the enumeration districts for the 1880, 1890 and 1900 censuses. These were used heavily in the research about LeDroit Park.

1901–3 Third Street NW, William and Arthur Birney

(Built 1887)

Another original McGill house, this structure is a duplex of two homes built for the Birney family. The side at number 1901 was the home of William Birney. Birney, born in Alabama to a former plantation owner turned antislavery advocate, was a staunch abolitionist.

Left: Birney residences on Cooper Circle, original McGill homes. *Author's collection.*

Right: Brevet Major General William Birney (circa 1861–65). *Library of Congress.*

During the Civil War, General Birney recruited free Black men to join the U.S. army. In the early years of the war, he fought at Manassas, Fredericksburg and Chancellorsville. During the second half of the war, he led men in the U.S. Colored Troops during the Siege of Petersburg and the Appomattox Campaign. Birney moved to Washington, D.C., in 1874 from Florida to start a law practice. He served as attorney general for the District of Columbia from 1876 to 1877.

His son Arthur Birney lived in the other side of the duplex. Arthur was born in France when his father was active in the French Revolution of 1848. The two Birneys had a law practice, Birney & Birney, near the U.S. Capitol. The younger served as the U.S. Attorney for the District of Columbia under President William McKinley in the 1890s.

Attorney General of D.C. (William Birney) and U.S. Attorney for D.C. (Arthur Birney) were two different positions. The U.S. Attorney is appointed by the president and represents the federal government in D.C. circuit cases. The Attorney General of D.C. represents the city in cases. When William Birney was attorney general, the position was appointed; today, it is an elected position.

1907 Third Street NW

(Original Demolished, Current Structure Built 1958)

While the building at number 1907 is new (or, rather, newer; it is from 1958), this was the site of an original McGill home. This was the residence of O.H. Irish and later Charles Darwin (no, not that one).

Orasmus H Irish

Orasmus H. Irish already had a long government career before he moved to Third Street NW in 1880. Though he was born and raised in New York City, Irish spent much of his early career in the western territories. He owned and edited a newspaper, was postmaster and an internal revenue collector in the Nebraska Territory. On behalf of the U.S. government, he was an "Indian agent" with the Omaha Reservation and superintendent of Indian affairs for Utah.

In Utah, he executed a treaty between the U.S. government and the Timpanagos Indians. There was an issue with the treaty when Brigham Young, leader of the Mormons, also signed it. Reporting on the treaty, Irish said of Congress: "Rather than associate with Brigham Young on such an occasion, they would have the negotiations fail; they would rather the Indians, than the Mormons, would have the land."

There was a rumor that Irish might be named governor of Utah, but critics claimed he was too friendly with the Mormons. He left Utah to serve as U.S. counsel to the Kingdom of Saxony (what is now part of unified Germany). After returning to the United States, he opened a plant nursery in Nebraska. It was destroyed by a swarm of locusts.

Contemporary sources refer to him as "Colonel Irish." This was likely an honorary title, as he has no record of military service.

Irish moved to Washington, D.C., in 1877 to work at the U.S. Bureau of Engraving and Printing. He was chief from 1878 until his death in 1883. The current bureau building on Fourteenth Street SW was built during his term. He was working in his office when he caught a cold due to a draft. A week later, he died in his home here in LeDroit Park. There was a debate as to whether the bureau should close for the funeral. But as bureau employees were paid by the day, the management did not want employees to be deprived of a whole day's work.

He was president of the LeDroit Park whist club. (Whist is a game similar to bridge.) The club delayed its weekly game after hearing of his death.

Charles C. Darwin

This building would later be home to Charles Carlyle Darwin. Along with his neighbor Henry Gannett, who lived a few houses down, Darwin worked at the newly established United States Geological Survey. When the USGS Library was established in 1882, he served as its first librarian. He worked with two other staff members and 1,400 books. He had a knowledge of many languages and was able to build up the USGS Library through international exchanges, making it one of the finest libraries of its kind. Darwin had worked at both the Library of Congress and the Smithsonian Institution Bureau of Ethnology, which was created to transfer records regarding American Indians from the Department of the Interior to the Smithsonian.

Darwin lived here with his wife, Gertrude Bascom. She was a graduate of Vassar College and had spent some time studying painting in Europe before marriage. She was a charter member of the Daughters of the American Revolution (number 168, to be exact). In the 1890s, she was librarian, then treasurer and historian of that organization and later vice-president of the Children of the American Revolution. She was treasurer of the DAR when the grounds for Constitution Hall was purchased, and her papers are sealed in the cornerstone of that building.

Her work as secretary of the Public Education Association of Washington

Portrait of Gertrude Bascom Darwin. Daughters of the American Revolution Magazine, *1915.*

helped lead to the creation of the Child Labor Bill. Later, Gertrude worked as a probation officer for the newly formed Juvenile Court. She helped organize the D.C. chapter of the National Association of Collegiate Alumni, aimed at providing postcollegiate opportunities to women who graduated from a four-year college course. The Washington branch, for which she served as the first secretary, helped reform sanitation in public schools in the city. But it also later resisted accepting LeDroit Park resident Mary Church Terrell as a member.

The Darwins lived here until 1892, when they left the changing neighborhood and moved to Georgetown.

1919 Third Street NW, Slowe Hall

(Built 1942)

Like many buildings in changing neighborhoods, what once was a historic site is now the location of apartments or condos. Slowe Hall was built in the 1940s.

Slowe Hall was built to house unmarried Black women working for the government during World War II. Along with its corresponding unit for men, Carver Hall, the federal dormitories were built to house over eight hundred workers. The complex had an infirmary, cafeteria, social center and recreation building. When it opened in 1943, single rooms were six dollars a week; double rooms were seven dollars a week. The dorm aimed to provide housing for those "government girls" working in D.C. for more than a year, not for short-term workers.

There were many dormitories built in Washington, D.C., for government workers. Others included Wake, Midway and Guam Halls. Wake and Guam were wood structures in Northeast D.C. and were always meant to be temporary. Midway Hall eventually closed. Slowe was the only female dormitory still open by 1948.

The building was designed by Hilyard Robinson. Robinson was a D.C. native who taught architecture at Howard University and designed many of

Exterior of Slowe Hall. *Author's collection.*

Staff of Lucy Diggs Slowe Hall in the lounge in 1942. *Library of Congress.*

the school's buildings. He is best known for designing the Langston Terrace Dwellings, one of the first federally funded housing projects.

When the dormitory opened in 1943, First Lady Eleanor Roosevelt and civil rights leader Mary McCleod Bethune were present for the ceremony. Roosevelt wrote about the project in her nationally syndicated column, My Day, where she mentions that "I also visited two permanent hotels, one for men and one for women, built by the government to meet the shortage in housing for colored government workers. It was encouraging to see them, because they are not only well built and tastefully decorated, but extremely well run."

The building was purchased by Howard University in 1948. The school turned it into an all-female dorm. It is named after Lucy Diggs Slowe. She was the first Black woman to be dean at an American university (Howard) and the first Black woman to win a professional sports title (tennis). Slowe lived nearby in Brookland with her long-term partner, playwright Mary P. Burrill.

In 2019, the university partnered with a developer to refurbish the buildings into non-university residential apartments.

Where Slowe Hall stands now was the site of three original McGill homes, 1913, 1915 and 1917 Third Street NW.

1913 Third Street NW

(Demolished)

There was an original McGill house at number 1913. An early resident was William A. Moorehead, a clerk in a government office. Other than his profession, there is not much in the historic record for Moorehead, except James McGill listing him in the *Architectural Advertiser* as a prominent resident of the neighborhood in the 1880s.

Later in the 1890s, Henry Durand lived here. Durand operated a fruit wholesale business on B Street NW (now Constitution Avenue NW). It was located next to the main downtown market, Center Market. According to advertisements, the company's specialties were apples and potatoes. Between 1890 and the early 1900s, LeDroit Park had a few fruit sellers. Around the same time, farther down Third Street NW toward Rhode Island Avenue NW, was another fruit wholesaler named Pulliam.

In the 1910s, this was the home of Dr. Simeon Carson, the Black physician whose private hospital was around the corner of Fourth Street NW.

1915 Third Street NW

(Demolished)

The most important of the McGill homes was his own. He lived at this location until his death in 1908, one of the last original LeDroit Park owners to remain in the neighborhood. McGill was born in Bowmanville, Ontario, Canada, to Irish parents. He listed his trade as "dealer in building offices."

Prior to working with Amzi Barber, McGill partnered with D.C. architect Henry R. Searle. Searle was the architect for the first main building of Howard University in 1867.

McGill designed most of the detached and semi-detached homes in the original suburb. Of the more than sixty homes built between 1873 and 1883, many remain standing. In 1875, McGill designed the Northern Liberty Market, which acted as D.C.'s convention hall in the first half of the twentieth century. That building, located near Fifth and K Street NW, was demolished in 1985.

McGill's career as an architect was short-lived and seems to have been limited to Washington, D.C. By the 1880s, he was working in the building supply trade but remained in his LeDroit Park home.

RESIDENCE OF MR. JAMES H. McGILL, LE DROIT PARK.

Drawing of James McGill's home, now demolished. The Slowe Hall building stands on the site today. *James H. McGill's architectural advisor, Printed Materials Collection, DC History Center.*

1917 THIRD STREET NW

(Demolished)

The building at 1917 housed a number of interesting families.

R.D. MUSSEY (RESIDED 1875–77)

Ruben D. Mussey arrived in Washington, D.C., to attend the 1861 inauguration of President Lincoln. When the American Civil War began, he immediately joined abolitionist Cassius Clay's militia, which guarded the White House. He eventually joined the army and recruited for the United States Colored Troops out of Nashville, Tennessee. There he met Vice President Andrew Johnson and, after Lincoln's assassination, returned to D.C. to serve President Johnson as his private secretary. During his short residency in LeDroit Park, Mussey was a private lawyer in a family firm with his wife, Ellen Spencer Mussey.

Above: Lawyer Ellen Spencer Mussey in 1900 in academic robe. *Library of Congress*.

Opposite: James Graydon (misspelled in this drawing) house, now demolished, was standing where Slowe Hall is today. *James H. McGill's architectural advisor, Printed Materials Collection, DC History Center*.

RESIDENCE OF LIEUT. JAS. GRADEN, U. S. N , LE DROIT PARK.

Ellen had not been formally educated as a lawyer, due to her gender. She was denied entry to National University and Columbian College (now George Washington University), so she taught herself with the assistance of her husband. After Ruben's death, she was granted special license to continue their law practice after passing an oral exam. She was later admitted to the bar of the U.S. Supreme Court. As a pioneer in legal education for women, Ellen and her colleague Emma Gillett (who graduated from Howard Law in 1883) opened the Women's Law Class in 1896. Two years later, this became Washington College of Law, the first law school founded by women in the world. Ellen was the dean until 1913.

The Musseys lived in LeDroit Park from 1875 to 1877. Ellen's brother Lyman Spencer lived just around the corner, at 502 T Street NW.

JAMES GRAYDON (RESIDED 1878–82)

James Graydon moved to LeDroit Park in 1875, living on T Street NW. By 1878, Graydon had moved into the house that was here with his wife, daughter, brother and his in-laws. He had been a lieutenant in the U.S. Navy during the Civil War. After the war, he was an inventor and engineer. He invented a carriage heater, a variety of explosives for military purposes

An 1896 postcard of the Earl's Court Giant Wheel, based on Lieutenant Graydon's design. *Author's collection.*

and a new compound turbine engine. The engine was so revolutionary that Andrew Carnegie planned to fit the engines to steamships and believed they could "cross the Atlantic in three days." (This is a feat that is not possible even today.)

Graydon's most relatable legacy is a giant amusement wheel. You may have seen it referred to as a Ferris wheel. The original Ferris wheel was designed in 1893 for the Chicago World's Fair. That same year, Graydon filed a patent for a similar type of amusement wheel. He would improve on his design and sell the patents to other engineers and contractors. Though not funded or built by Graydon, the Gigantic Wheel of Earl's Court, London; the one in Blackpool, England; and the one built for the 1900 Paris Exposition were all Graydon wheels. The only Graydon wheel still standing today is Vienna's Prater Wheel.

Unless you're an engineer or an expert in giant wheels, you may not notice the difference between Graydon and Ferris wheels. The inner and outer rims of Graydon wheels are much closer together than those in a Ferris wheel. Graydon used a different type of motor and wire mechanism to spin it, and he included observation decks that could be accessed by stairs in the middle.

Graydon also patented a ride that was essentially a giant tower in which passenger cars traveled up and down on a spiral track.

By 1883, James Graydon had moved. His brother William, a clerk at the U.S. Patent Office, stayed in LeDroit Park but moved to a house on the northwestern part of Anna Julia Cooper Circle that has since been demolished.

William W. Dudley (Resided 1882–87)

William Wade Dudley lived here for five years while serving as commissioner of pensions under Presidents James A. Garfield and Chester A. Arthur.

Dudley had served in the U.S. Army in the famed Iron Brigade, where he led his regiment at the Battles of Antietam and Gettysburg. His leg had to be amputated in the field at Gettysburg.

Dudley left politics the same year he left LeDroit Park. In the 1888 election for the Republican nomination for president between Benjamin Harrison and Grover Cleveland, Dudley sent a letter discussing purchasing votes in Indiana. This letter was leaked and would lead to secret ballots in the United States. Prior to this, ballots were printed by political parties with votes filled in beforehand and voters could choose their party's ballot to submit.

Langston Hughes (Resided 1924)

In 1924, poet Langston Hughes moved to Washington, D.C. His mother and half-brother had moved to the city to live with cousins at 1917 Third Street NW. The cousins were Ralph and Anne Langston, son and daughter-in-law of John Mercer Langston, who lived on the Howard University campus.

In his autobiography, *The Big Sea*, Hughes writes:

> *I am sure I did not look like a distinguished poet, when I walked up to my cousin's porch in Washington's Negro society section, LeDroit Park, next door to the famous-colored surgeon and heart specialist, Dr. Carson.*
>
> *Listen, everybody! Never go to live with relatives if you're broke! That is an error. My cousins introduced me as just back from Europe, but they didn't say I came by chipping decks on a freight ship—which seemed to me an essential explanation.*

Hughes did not live here long before moving to other parts of Washington, D.C.

208 T Street NW

(Built 1893)

In the 1890s, two future brothers-in-law lived here in 208 T Street NW while working at the U.S. Geological Survey.

Van H. Manning was the son of a Confederate colonel and Mississippi representative of the same name. The younger Manning was a civil engineer until 1910, when he began working at the U.S. Bureau of Mines. As director of that organization, he began researching toxic gas for use in warfare and established chemical laboratories that would be used during World War I. He believed chemical research should not be controlled by the military, but President Wilson created the Chemical Warfare Service during the war. Manning's wife, Emily, was active in his work at the Bureau of Mines, assisting with rescue methods.

Manning lived here with Louis C. Fletcher, who would later marry Manning's sister. Fletcher was a topographer and geologist with the USGS. He led several expeditions that were the first to summit new peaks. Dickerman

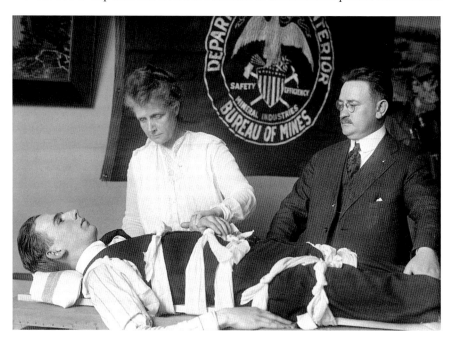

Emily Manning demonstrating rescue methods at the U.S. Bureau of Mines *Library of Congress.*

Mountain, Vesper Peak and Hermans Peak are all in the mountain ranges north of Seattle, Washington. Fletcher claimed to have been among the first expeditions to the top.

210 T Street NW

(Built 1893)

The house at 210 T Street NW is still a bed-and-breakfast in 2022, fitting for its history as an occasional guest house. While this was the home of the Perry family in the early 1900s, rooms were sometimes let out to performers at the nearby Howard Theatre.

When the Howard Theatre opened in 1910 on Florida Avenue NW at the other end of T Street, Black performers were not allowed to stay at most of the hotels in the city. Some of the families in LeDroit Park opened rooms for the artists to stay in while in town. Geneva Perry's family, which lived at this house, was one of them. The introductions to musicians in her childhood may have helped encourage her love of music.

A 1940s album of the International Sweethearts of Rhythm. *Author's collection.*

Geneva played the saxophone and in the 1940s performed with the International Sweethearts of Rhythm, an all-female, mixed-race big band. After graduating from Virginia State University, Perry joined the touring ensemble. They played the Howard Theatre and the Apollo Theater in New York and toured until 1949 as one of the best female bands. She was nicknamed "Teacher" and would go on to teach music in North Carolina. In her later years, she returned to LeDroit Park. She was active in the preservation of the neighborhood and established a bed-and-breakfast at this house.

201 T Street NW, Anna Julia Cooper

(Built 1876)

Anna Julia Cooper lived in this house from 1916 until her death in 1964. There is too much to summarize about her incredible 106 years of life. She was born into slavery in North Carolina and started her education at the age of 9. She excelled and began teaching herself. After being widowed at the age of 21, she attended Oberlin College. Through the late 1800s, Cooper taught and continued her own education. In 1888, she earned a master's degree from Oberlin, becoming one of the first two Black women to earn an MA. Her classmates and future LeDroit Park neighbors Mary Church Terrell and Ida Gibbs were also among the first Black female college graduates.

In 1892, she moved to Washington, D.C. She taught at M Street / Dunbar High School, becoming its principal. Her focus was on classical rather than vocational education, and during her tenure, many graduates went on to Ivy League schools.

She published her seminal work, *A Voice from the South,* calling for women's rights and civil rights, in 1892. It is considered the first work of Black feminism and is the most famous of her many works.

When she took custody of her late brother's five children, she had been a PhD candidate at Columbia University. She purchased this house to accommodate her new larger family and paused her doctoral studies. It was only a pause. She successfully defended her thesis, "The Attitude of France on the Question of Slavery Between 1789 and 1848," in 1925 at the University of Paris–Sorbonne. She became only the fourth Black American woman to earn a PhD.

Author and educator Anna Julia Cooper in her home on T Street NW. *Scurlock Studio Records, Archives Center, National Museum of American History, Smithsonian Institution.*

This house was not just her family home. Cooper was dedicated to education for all, and in the 1930s, she opened her home to students at Frelinghuysen University for classes. Frelinghuysen University had been founded by Rosetta Lawson in 1917 as a night school for Black working-class adults who wanted to continue their education beyond public school. While Cooper was president, the school moved into this home to continue

Exterior of Anna Julia Cooper's home. *Author's collection.*

offering classes. Like her belief at M Street / Dunbar School, Cooper was determined to provide more than vocational training.

Cooper dedicated her life to education for all. In the official U.S. passport, of the twelve quotes included, only one is from a woman. Cooper wrote, "The cause of freedom is not the cause of a race or a sect, a party or a class—it is the cause of humankind, the very birthright of humanity."

3

T Street NW
(Maple Avenue)

T Street NW was originally called Maple Avenue. In the few blocks running from Sixth Street to Second Street NW, nearly every house was home to someone worthy of inclusion. The "T Street Elites," both in the original gated community and later when LeDroit Park was predominately Black, lived in original McGill homes and in the 1880 row houses that quickly filled in the open lots.

326 T NW, MARY CHURCH AND ROBERT TERRELL

(Built 1887)

In the 1970s, a fire destroyed half of this duplex. The remaining side had been the home to Mary Church Terrell and her husband, Robert Terrell. As of 2022, the Howard University–owned house was being renovated and restored, with the hopes of turning it into a resource center and space dedicated to the legacy of the Terrells.

Mary Church Terrell was born in Memphis, Tennessee, to a self-made real estate millionaire. Her father, Robert Church, is considered the first Black American millionaire in the South and would eventually own most of Memphis. Her mother, Louisa, owned a successful hair salon—one of the first Black women to do so, at a time when women of any race were not entrepreneurs. Mary followed in her parents' footsteps of breaking barriers.

Above: Terrell House, 326 T Street NW, 1933. *Historic American Buildings Survey*.

Opposite: Author and activist Mary Church Terrell between 1880 and 1900. *Library of Congress*.

She graduated from Oberlin in 1884, one of the first Black women to graduate college with a four-year bachelor's degree. Other Black women in that graduating class would also live in LeDroit Park. Four years later, again with Cooper, Mary became one of the first two Black women to earn a master's degree.

Throughout her life, Mary was a forerunner in the suffrage movement for Black women. She was fluent in several languages and went on the speaking circuit. When she addressed the International Congress of Women in 1904 in Berlin, Germany, she presented her speech in English, French and German. She published in several journals and wrote an autobiography, *A Colored Woman in a White World* (1940). She was offered the job as registrar at Oberlin, which would have made her the first Black woman in that position, but she declined.

Mary spent much of her adult life fighting for civil rights. She helped with the court cases that led to the desegregation of D.C. restaurants. She was a charter member of the NAACP, the National Association of College Women and the National Association of Colored Women.

Like many LeDroit Park residents in the early 1900s, she was involved with M Street / Dunbar High School. It was here that she met Robert Terrell. When they married, Mary had to resign as a teacher, as that position was restricted to unmarried women. Only four years later, she was appointed to the school board of Washington, D.C., the first Black woman to be on a school board of a major city.

Robert's family had moved from southern Virginia to D.C. after the end of the Civil War. While he did not grow up as a millionaire, Robert did have a well-off and well-connected family. His father served as the personal valet for General Ulysses S Grant. Terrell attended the private prep Groton School in Massachusetts and later Harvard University. While teaching at M Street / Dunbar High School, he earned his law degree from Howard University.

Robert left the high school to serve in the federal government. In 1901, he was appointed justice of the peace in D.C. (the second Black man to hold that position). Ten years later, President William Howard Taft named him to the Municipal Court of D.C. Robert and the three other Black men appointed to high office under Taft were known as his "Black Cabinet."

The Terrells were among the early Black residents of LeDroit Park. In 1894, they purchased a house on Fourth Street. Due to the racism at the time, they had to use a straw buyer—a white friend purchased the house and then immediately sold it to them.

They moved to this house in 1898, where Mary remained until her death in 1954, just two months after witnessing the U.S. Supreme Court's decision in *Brown v. Board of Education*, which ended racial segregation in schools, a cause she had spent her life fighting for.

330 T Street NW

(Built 1880)

In 1880, this house was built for Charles A. White. While it's not recorded that it was designed by James McGill, it is a reasonable assumption.

Charles A. White

Charles grew up in rural Iowa Territory with a love of geology and nature, but he did not have the finances to pursue these interests as a career. After working as a medical doctor, he began focusing on geology and found success despite no formal education in the subject.

In 1866, he became the state geologist for Iowa, a position that would eventually lead him to Washington, D.C., to work with the Smithsonian Institution and the U.S. Geological Survey with his neighbors Henry Gannett and Charles C. Darwin. When White moved to LeDroit Park, he lived a few houses down T Street NW before having this house built.

You can see his work with invertebrate fossils in the National Fossil Collection at the Smithsonian Natural History Museum on the National Mall.

301 T Street NW, former home of Fountain Peyton and Charles A. White. *Author's collection.*

Fountain Peyton

In 1908, White sold his house to Fountain Peyton. Peyton was born enslaved in 1861 in Virginia. When his father was taken south by the Confederate army, his mother escaped to the contraband camps in D.C. with him as a baby.

Peyton pursued an education starting at the age of six, proving to be a bright student. He supported himself by selling newspapers, often selling to President Grant, who was known to be a good tipper to the newsboys. At the time, Howard University required study in classical languages to enroll, which Peyton did not have. Undeterred in his ambition to be a lawyer, Peyton taught at a school in Maryland while studying to apply again.

His acceptance to Howard Law School came at the same time as his job as a postman. He attended lectures at school with his mailbag and then ran the route to ensure the mail was delivered on schedule.

His law practice in D.C. opened in 1890, and he became a successful criminal defense attorney. Peyton was the first Black lawyer to argue at the D.C. Court of Appeals and the first Black examiner in chancery for D.C. He followed in his neighbor's path and was appointed to D.C.'s school board in 1915, just a few years after Mary Church Terrell left the position.

In the dining room at this house, Peyton pursued two unique hobbies. He particularly enjoyed dismantling and reassembling radios. He also enjoyed doing his own historical research. Ira Frederick Aldridge was a Black Shakespearian actor in Europe in the 1820s–60s. Peyton published a book about Aldridge in 1917. It was printed by Robert Lewis Pendleton, one of the first Black printers to establish a printing company in Washington, D.C.

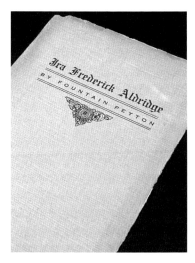

The book, *A Glance at the Life of Ira Aldridge*, is a unique combination of a book about a Black actor, written by a Black author, printed by a Black printer in the early twentieth century.

Fountain Peyton's *A Glance at the Life of Ira Frederick Aldridge*, printed in 1917. *Photo by Aaron Rinca, current owner of Peyton's home.*

400 T Street NW, Edmund Woog

(Built 1886)

Edmund Woog was a German immigrant who lived in LeDroit Park in the 1890s. Woog immigrated to America in the 1850s and joined the New York Sixty-Eighth Regiment Volunteer Infantry in July 1861 during the Civil War. While serving the U.S. Army at the Battle of Manassas in 1862, Woog was shot in the lower jaw. He suffered greatly from this. He lost his ability to speak clearly and chew his food properly, and he lost some of his sight. He had been studying to be a lawyer before the war, but his injury and inability to speak clearly affected that ambition. He was still able to work in the legal field as chief clerk in the adjutant general's office in Missouri. His report on the Ku Klux Klan in Missouri is what encouraged the governor to utilize state militia and local law enforcement to curtail Klan activity in 1871.

When he moved to Washington, D.C., Woog worked at the Bureau of Indian Affairs, becoming the chief of the finance office. The first house the Woog family lived in was 416 U Street NW. Their son was possibly born in that house in 1879, but by 1881, they had moved to Fourth Street. Farther down Fourth Street toward Florida Avenue NW, there were some original McGill stand-alone houses on the left. The Woogs lived there for the first few years of their son Benjamin's life before moving into the house here on the corner of Fourth and T Street NW. They had this house at 400 T Street NW built in 1886.

Benjamin Woog was a journalist and a U.S. Marine. He started out as the Washington correspondent for the *Nashville Banner*, assigned to the press gallery of the U.S. Capitol. In 1898, during the Spanish-American War, he enlisted with the U.S. First Cavalry as part of Teddy Roosevelt's Rough Riders. He never made it up San Juan Hill, as he was a member of one of the four companies left behind in Tampa due to insufficient storage. He was later sent to the Philippines. Here he wrote a letter to Teddy Roosevelt, whom he addressed as "my dear Colonel," and spoke on friendly terms about a recommendation for a promotion.

Woog fought with Colonel George Elliot at Novelta in the Philippines and then was stationed aboard the USS *Buffalo*, USS *San Francisco* and USS *Chicago*. In 1905, he failed to be promoted and was discharged. He moved to New York City and was killed in a car crash in 1908. At this point, Woog was a prominent New York real estate agent, and the car was being driven

Headquarters, First Regiment Marines,

Cavite, P.I. December 20, 1900.

My dear Colonel:-

Sometimes I think one can worry even his friends too
much but I do hope I am not found doing that.

There seems a great probability to us out here that the
Quartermasters Department of the Marine Corps will be increased
by the addition of several Captains and Assistant Quartermasters.
These are surely needed, and if this increase is granted, I
would like very much to be appointed.   I am now one of the senior
first lieutenants of the Corps, being #12, and I hardly think
any of my seniors will want the billet.   Will you please see the
General (Heywood) for me, also Secretary Long, and speak a good
word.   I am sure that you will.

Please give my compliments to Mrs. Roosevelt.   I hope
that your coming sojourn in Washington will be a pleasant one ,
and that you will enjoy good health.

Very sincerely and respectfully,

Benjamin B Woog

First Lieutenant, U.S.Marine Corps.

5859

Letter from Benjamin Woog to Teddy Roosevelt, asking for a recommendation for a
promotion, written from the Philippines during the Spanish-American War. *Library of Congress.*

by his chauffeur. There was a break in the steering gear, and the car crashed into the woods.

Prominent Washington architect Edmund Woog Dreyfuss is the grandson of Edmund Woog. Dreyfuss's mother, Malvine, lived at 400 T Street NW before her marriage.

In 1985, Reverend Jesse Jackson purchased the house. At this point, it was one of the homes that Howard University owned. He had been a candidate for the Democratic presidential nomination the year before and would be again in the next election. When Jackson purchased the house, it had been boarded up and abandoned. Renovations took place shortly after. This was to be his second home, since he spent so much time in Washington, D.C. He still owns the house as of 2022.

401 T NW

(Built 1913)

In the 1942 *Who's Who in Colored America*, Roy W. Tibbs is listed here at 401 T Street NW. Tibbs is most often remembered by the Evan-Tibbs House, not far away on Vermont Avenue NW. However, he left that house in the 1920s. For much of his later life, Tibbs lived on the Howard University campus at 601 Howard Place.

Tibbs graduated from Fisk University and moved to D.C. by 1912. He was professor of piano and organ at Howard University. Like many Howard professors, his personal education continued during his teaching career. While at Howard, Tibbs earned advanced degrees from the Oberlin Conservatory of Music. He traveled to Paris to study with French pianist Isador Phillip until World War I broke out.

By the 1920s, he had founded the Howard Glee Club and was its conductor. He had also married Lillian Evans. She was a renowned opera singer, more famous in Europe, where she found less racism and segregation. She performed under the stage name Madame Evanti. Roy and Lillian divorced. She continued her music career, and he continued teaching at Howard.

Interestingly, the 1942 *Who's Who in Colored America*, which lists Tibbs, does not include the world-famous opera singer Lillian Evans.

408 T Street NW,
Bennetta Bullock and Walter Washington

(Built 1895)

Though this house is known as the "Home to Walter Washington," it was first the home to the Bullock family. Reverend George Oliver Bullock was a Baptist minister in North Carolina before moving his family to Washington, D.C., in 1918 to serve as pastor of the Third Baptist Church. The family had eight children.

One son, Dr. Samuel Bullock, became a noted psychiatrist in Philadelphia. He was the only Black graduate in the 1943 undergraduate class at Dartmouth and in the 1946 class of New York University College of Medicine. Another son, William H. Bullock, was a physician and professor at Howard University Medical School. He opened a practice here at the family home in 1950, which he operated until 1990. The medical sign on the porch column can still be seen today.

A daughter, Bennetta, earned a PhD from Catholic University in counseling psychology. She taught, was principal of Cardozo High School in D.C., directed the Cardozo Project in Urban Education and served on the Presidential Commission of Juvenile Delinquency. From 1964 until 1981, she worked in the U.S. Department of Labor, focusing on education and jobs for women. During this time, she was also the First Lady of Washington D.C.

Bennetta married Walter Washington in 1941. Washington had arrived in D.C. to attend Howard University for undergraduate studies and law school. Though his public-service record includes supervising D.C.'s Alley Dwelling Authority, the National Capital Housing Authority and the Housing Authority of New York City, he is most known for being mayor of Washington.

First mayor of Washington, D.C., Walter Washington, 1968. *Library of Congress.*

Without getting too much into the politics of D.C. statehood, in 1967, President Lyndon Johnson reorganized local D.C. politics from a three-person commissioner government to a mayor-commissioner form of government. Walter Washington was appointed the first mayor-commissioner of D.C., serving until 1974. When D.C. was given home rule and the right to elect its own mayor, Washington was elected as the first mayor of D.C. since 1871 and the first Black mayor of a major American city.

He lived at the Bullock family home from the time of his marriage to Bennetta in 1941 to her death in 1991, when he purchased the house next door and combined the two into one home.

Dr. Bennetta Bullock and Walter Washington were both invested in their neighborhood. Their time in LeDroit Park corresponds with the beginning of its midcentury decline. Overcrowding was an issue; racism and disinterest from the city government was another. As leaders of the LeDroit Park Civic Association—the same one once led by white males of the early neighborhood—the Washingtons helped promote a focus on safety and opportunity.

413 T Street NW, West A. Hamilton

(Built 1901)

Throughout his life, West Alexander Hamilton was referred to as "Colonel." He was technically a brigadier general, the first person in the National Guard to receive that rank. This rank was given to him at the age of ninety-six after a lifelong career in the armed forces. He alternated between careers in the military and in education. West was at the Mexican border in 1916 with the Buffalo Soldiers during World War I and in North Africa and Italy during World War II.

Between military service, he was an educator. Hamilton served on D.C.'s board of education for twenty-one years, taught in D.C. schools for ten years and earned a master's degree from American University at the age of sixty-nine.

In addition to being a teacher and a military man, West was an entrepreneur. He and his brother owned and operated the Hamilton Printing Company from 1910 to the 1970s. They published a weekly newspaper, the *Sentinel*. In his role as publisher, he was invited to speak in Congress in 1928 along with his mother, activist Julia West Hamilton, and his neighbor Mary

Church Terrell. The Committee on Public Buildings and Grounds held a hearing to establish a building as "a tribute to the Negro's Contribution to the Achievements of America." Hamilton said to the committee:

We ought to have something to remind the new and present generation of negros of our achievements. They come along and, under the bar sinister of being negroes, which is upon them, they need something to encourage them....It will hasten the day when the negroes will take their place as rightful citizens, and it will hasten the day when there will be no class distinction in America, and the only requirement of citizenship will be that measure of standard set for everybody else in this country.

The resolution to create a tribute was signed by President Calvin Coolidge in 1929 but stalled afterward. None of the speakers in favor that day would live to see what eventually came from their testimony. The National Museum of African American History and Culture opened on the National Mall in 2016.

The West A. Hamilton National Guard Museum at the D.C. Armory is named in his honor. He lived in this house in the 1920s–40s, just around the corner from his mother. Julia West Hamilton lived at 320 U Street from 1918 to 1937. She had been a founder and president of the Phyllis Wheatley YMCA, an activist against police brutality in the 1930s and a member and leader in numerous social, charitable and civil rights clubs and organizations.

412–14 T Street NW, Charles Syphax and Ernest Just

(Built 1889)

In 1920, Ernest Everett Just (at 412) and Charles Sumner Syphax (at 414) were briefly neighbors.

Just had graduated from Dartmouth, where he had earned nearly ever honor possible. He came to teach at Howard—no matter how brilliant and skilled, Black men had trouble finding employment at white universities. He would eventually became the head of the new Department of Zoology at Howard, a position he held until his death in 1941. He moved into this house in 1914 with his first wife, Ethel Highwarden, a German teacher at Howard.

Residences of neighbors Ernest Everett Just and Charles Sumner Syphax. *Author's collection.*

Just is considered one of the first world-renowned Black scientists. He was the first recipient of the NAACP Spingarn Medal and the first American of any race to be invited to the Kaiser Wilhelm Institute in Berlin, the research home of many Nobel Prize recipients at the time.

Just spent a lot of his later years in Europe, but his first wife and their children remained in this house through the 1940s.

Charles Sumner Syphax lived in three different houses on T Street NW. When Just moved into 412 T in 1914, Syphax was living one block down. Syphax would move to this house at number 414 by 1920.

A son of the prominent Syphax family, Charles Sumner was a math professor at Howard University for forty-six years. It was also at Howard that he earned bachelor of arts, bachelor of law and master of law degrees. Beginning in 1914, he was dean of Howard Academy, the secondary school associated with the university, until it closed in 1919.

Biologist Dr. Ernest Everett Just, circa 1920. *National Portrait Gallery*.

The Syphax family was descended from Martha Washington. Her grandson George Washington Parks Custis forced himself onto a house maid, who then had a daughter, Mariah, Charles Sumner's grandmother. The Syphax family would own much of what is now the western part of Arlington National Cemetery, which had been Freedman's Village, established by the Syphax family. Charles Sumner's uncle William was the first chairman of the D.C. Board of Trustees of Colored Public Schools, which established M Street / Dunbar High School, the first Black high school and the alma mater of much of LeDroit Park.

420 T Street NW, Nelson Weatherless

(Built 1886)

Nelson Weatherless graduated from high school at the age of fourteen. When he attended Howard University, he earned the prizes for highest average for four years in mathematics, physics and Greek. He headed the physics department at M Street School and made sure its successor school, Dunbar, had excellent laboratories in its new facility.

Weatherless was also a lawyer and served as chief examiner on the D.C. Board of Examiners. He sued the New Grand Opera House in Washington, D.C., for violating civil rights by segregating the seating in the theater.

421 T Street NW, Benjamin Butterworth

(Built 1876)

This original McGill home was built in 1876 for Benjamin Butterworth of Ohio. It is an interesting aside that Butterworth moved into a community that did not welcome Black residents. His family, plantation owners in Virginia in the 1810s, freed their slaves, moved to Ohio and ran a prominent station on the Underground Railroad. Butterworth Station was run by his grandfather, also named Benjamin. His father, William, helped freedom seekers to the next station.

Before moving to D.C., Butterworth was a lawyer, U.S. district attorney and state senator in Ohio. Butterworth served in the U.S. Congress as representative from Ohio in the 1880s, was a regent of the Smithsonian

Portrait of Benjamin Butterworth, circa 1898. History of the Republican Party in Ohio.

Institution and secretary and solicitor general of the 1893 Chicago World's Fair. Most notably, he was commissioner of patents from 1896 until his death two years later.

In 1890, his daughter Mary left the family home here, expecting to move to a new house with her new husband. Mary was engaged to a dispatch agent from New York City named Haughwout Howe. He arrived from New York a few days before the scheduled wedding day and suffered a debilitating attack from a chronic illness. The wedding was held earlier than planned. In the span of twenty-two hours, Mary went from betrothed, to bride, to widow. Howe died at nearly the same time that the wedding was originally scheduled. Mary returned to the LeDroit Park home.

Colored YWCA

(Demolished)

What is now a vacant lot and abandoned playground from the closed Howard University Hospital Child Care Center was an original McGill double home.

By 1879, one side of the house was the home of Charles A. White before he moved to 330 T Street NW. The other side was home to Grove K. Gilbert, who had been living at the corner of Sixth and T Street NW.

Gilbert lived in LeDroit Park for a short time (1875–80). Like many of the early LeDroit Park residents, he was a geologist and worked for the U.S. Geological Survey after its creation. Gilbert's work focused on planetary science as well as the study of landscape evolution. There are craters on the moon and Mars named after him.

When Gilbert left, he moved to Corcoran Street NW near Logan Circle. Moving from that same block of Corcoran Street NW to LeDroit Park, Sumner Increase Kimball moved into this house.

Kimball was chief of the U.S. Treasury Department's Revenue Marine Division. From this position, he worked with Congress to consolidate the system of lifesaving stations that had been built in the previous decades

RESIDENCES OF MR. E. K. GILBERT AND DR. CHAS. WHITE,
LE DROIT PARK.

Drawing of the original home on T Street NW on the same lot that became 429 T Street NW, possibly the building that was used as the Colored YWCA in the 1910s. *James H. McGill's architectural advisor, Printed Materials Collection, DC History Center.*

Part of the 1919–21 Baist Real Estate map, showing the "Colored YWCA" located at 429 T Street NW before it moved to Ninth and Rhode Island Avenue NW. *Library of Congress.*

on the New England coast. This became a government agency called the United States Life-Saving Service. He served as its superintendent until it became the United States Coast Guard in 1915. Kimball stayed in LeDroit Park only until 1891, when he moved back to Logan Circle.

In the first decade of the twentieth century, the road name was changed from Maple to T Street NW, and the house number of this building changed from 409–11 to 429. The property was purchased for $4,300 by a group of Black women to be the first permanent quarters of Washington's YWCA for "Colored Women."

In 1905, Rosetta Lawson, the same person who founded Frelinghuysen University, and her "Booklovers Club" formed a D.C. chapter of the YWCA. This was the first in D.C. and the only Black independent YCWA in the United States. In 1910, they purchased this ten-bedroom house at 429 T Street NW.

Julia West Hamilton, whose son Colonel West A. Hamilton lived one block away, was its third and longest-serving president. Julia Cooper and Mary Church Terrell were also members.

The "Colored" YWCA, as it is noted on maps of the time, was located here until 1920, when it moved to nearby Ninth and Rhode Island Avenue NW. Renamed the Phyllis Wheatley YWCA, it remains a part of the community to this day.

507 T Street NW

(Built 1870s)

The eastern half of this unique-looking duplex is an original McGill, built by at least 1879. The western half would have been the other half of the duplex, but the current structure was built in 1929.

Early residents of the two homes were Arnold B. Johnson and Ellery C. Ford. Ford lived in the one that has since been replaced with a modern home. He was a colonel in the Fifth Regiment of the United States Colored Troops (all officers in the USCT were white). He fought at the Battle of Chaffin's Farm next to Christian Fleetwood, a Black soldier who moved to LeDroit Park in the next decade.

Arnold B. Johnson lived in the remaining half of the house. He was the chief clerk of the Lighthouse Establishment, which operated under the U.S. Department of the Treasury to maintain all government lighthouses in the nation.

"Sunrise or sunset, own a Liberty Bond" by artist Eugenie DeLand. United States, 1917. *Library of Congress.*

The Deland family moved in to 507 T Street NW in the first decade of the 1900s. Theodore Deland worked at the Treasury Department for forty years. He earned the respect of Teddy Roosevelt, who once requested him personally at a meeting. He worked on the loans for the Spanish-American War and later the Panama Canal bonds. He literally worked himself to death on the latter. After thirty-six straight hours working day and night on calculations for the loans, Theodore said he was going to take a little rest and died a few hours later. After his death, the family left this house.

His daughter Eugenie lived here with the family before her father's death. Eugenie was an accomplished artist and art teacher. As a student at Drexel Institute of Art, she studied under illustrator Howard Pyle and graduated in the same class as Maxfield Parrish. She taught at the Corcoran School of Art and nearby McKinley Tech High School. She painted the ceiling of the National Headquarters of the Order of the Eastern Star and did the art for numerous publications for the Treasury Department.

In 1917, she was the only female artist whose submission was accepted to design a war bond during World War I. Five hundred thousand copies of her design were printed to encourage the purchase of liberty bonds. Some of the posters she designed were sent to General John Pershing in France. It would be the first time that a poster advertising war bonds was distributed on the front lines. The hope was that this would encourage soldiers that the American public was financing their efforts. Eugenie would end up designing two posters for the effort.

Eugenie Deland wasn't the only artist to walk these halls. For the second half of the twentieth century, this was known as the House of Secrets, a speakeasy of sorts—not so much in the style of a Prohibition-era speakeasy, but more that it was an unlicensed nightclub.

In 1998, there was such a loud party that neighbors complained to the mayor:

We also have a problem with the parties held in our neighborhood at an after-hours nightclub, the House of Secrets. It's no secret that the last two times The Artist Formerly Known as Prince performed in the area, he had a party that went on from 1 a.m. until 5 a.m. on a Tuesday morning. The purple buses roared down our one-way street and unloaded noisy passengers. The limousines, cars and taxis pulled up, double parked and blocked our driveways. How is it that an after-hours establishment is allowed to exist in our neighborhood? We, law-abiding citizens, do not want this nightclub. We do not want to party. We want to sleep.

500, 502 and 504 T Street NW

(Built in 1876)

The first two houses on the corner, 500 and 502, are original to the neighborhood and are the designs of James McGill. They were built in the 1870s.

Number 500 was first home to Lyman P. Spencer. He was a penman. Spencer wrote a book expanding on the Spencerian system of penmanship devised by his father, Platt Rogers Spencer. Spencerian was the de facto script for businesses before the typewriter. If you're not sure what it looks like, the Coca-Cola logo is in Spencerian.

Next door at 502 was the home of Samuel Swimfin Burdett. Burdett had immigrated to Ohio from England at the age of twelve. His first time living in D.C. was as a representative from Missouri, but he returned in 1874 as commissioner of the General Land Office, the bureau that managed public lands. He lived in LeDroit Park for a few years before moving to M Street NW and then to Virginia. In 1914, he returned to his boyhood home in England for a visit. There, he had a sudden illness and died in the same room in which he was born. He is buried in Arlington National Cemetery, having served in the U.S. Army in the Civil War.

Note the sign still on the side of 502 T Street NW. James Walker purchased the house at 502 in the 1930s and operated his dental practice here.

James Walker Jr. was the son of Major James Walker and nephew-in-law to Arthur Newman. These two men lived next door. They had married sisters, Jennie and Beatrice Johnson. From 1905 to the early 1910s, the Walkers and Newmans lived around the corner on Fourth Street. They would continue to live together when they moved to 504 T Street NW by 1915.

In 1912, Major James Walker became battalion commander of the First Separate Battalion of the D.C. National Guard. That year, he became supervising principal in the D.C. school system. He had been principal of the Syphax School, named for William Syphax, uncle of neighbor Charles Sumner Syphax. Educator and military man, Walker was committed to both. The First Separate Battalion was one of the first Black military units. It began as the Washington Cadet Corps in 1867, formed by future LeDroit Park resident Christian Fleetwood.

In June 1916, the First Separate Battalion was one of the first troops sent to the Mexican border during Pancho Villa's revolution. Shortly after, it was the first National Guard unit called into federal service to protect the nation's capital with the threat of World War I.

Left: The James E. Walker medical sign can still be seen on the front of his residence, next door to the home of his father, Major James E. Walker. *Author's collection*.

Below: Sixteen members of the First Separate Battalion of the Washington National Guard. Arthur Newman is standing in the center. *DC History Center*.

Walker and the First Separate Battalion guarded the city's waterways, railroads and public buildings. When his men were sent to Europe, Walker was sent west to recover from tuberculous. He never did and died in 1918, becoming the first member of the D.C. military forces to die during World War I. The First Separate Battalion learned of his death while aboard a ship bound for the front lines. They fought with the French army's Red Hand Division, suffering many casualties because they refused to surrender or give up the fight. Major James E. Walker is buried at Arlington National Cemetery.

Walker's daughter Beatrice L. Walker continued the family tradition of education. She graduated from M Street / Dunbar High School, Miner Teacher's College and Howard University. She earned a master of education degree from Harvard University in 1945, only twenty years after the first Black female graduate of Harvard's School of Education.

D.C.'s American Legion Post 26 was named in his honor and counted among its members his brother-in-law Captain Arthur Newman and neighbor Colonel West Alexander Hamilton.

Arthur Newman answered similar calls to teach and serve. Newman was principal of Armstrong Tech High School and served in World War I and commanded the First Separate Battalion.

517 T Street NW

(Built 1874)

The cottage at 517 T Street NW is a favorite of the original McGill homes. Its bright colors would have been standard at the turn of the twentieth century, though it is unique in the neighborhood today.

The home was built by McGill in 1874 as one of the earliest homes. An early resident was Joseph B. Marvin, who at the time was a clerk in the Internal Revenue Service. Joseph Badger Marvin was an interesting person who mostly advertised his address as Lock Box 379 in the Corcoran Building, which stood at Fifteenth and Pennsylvania Avenue NW but has since been torn down.

Marvin ran the Bureau of General Information, an official-sounding but not government-related entity. He advertised through publications in 1887 that if anyone was looking for information or research assistance in places like the Smithsonian, the National Archives or the Library of Congress, they could send one dollar to the lockbox for him to find the answer.

The Bureau of General Information,

Joseph P. Marvin, Manager,

(Assisted by Experts in all Branches.)

Office in the Corcoran Building, Opposite the Treasury.

P. O. LOCK BOX 379.   **WASHINGTON, D. C.**

Literary, Scientific, and Medical Authorities consulted. Transcripts and Translations furnished. Bibliography of all Literature obtained. Legislation reported. Information obtained from the Departments. Applications for Public Documents attended to.

QUESTIONS UPON ALL SUBJECTS ANSWERED.

People desiring Information from Washington will no longer be obliged to take the time, and impose upon the good nature, of their friends in this city, but, by applying directly to the BUREAU OF GENERAL INFORMATION, their wishes will be promptly attended to.

The circulars and cards of the Bureau will be forwarded to any address upon ;equest, and citizens of Washington will do themselves and their correspondents a service by referring them to this Bureau.

Terms—A fee of one dollar for every question.

One dollar an hour for Research, 10 cents a folio for Transcripts, 30 cents a folio for Translations.

Advertisement of Joseph Marvin's Bureau of General Information. *Summer 1887 edition of "Public Opinion."*

Marvin then worked in the U.S. Patent Office as a draftsman from 1888 to 1893, when he was forced to resign, possibly at the behest of Josiah Quincy, former mayor of Boston and at the time assistant secretary of state. There was an issue of Quincy's new lithographic company competing with a local company, and Marvin may or may not have been sabotaging the new company. A congressional hearing was held regarding the drama.

Other than a note in McGill's *Architectural Advertiser* that he lived in this house in the 1870s, there is no record of how long he was in LeDroit Park. Marvin must have been elsewhere by 1880, as journalist George Kennan lived in this house.

George Kennan was an explorer and journalist known for his expertise on Russia. He spent a lot of time surveying Siberia for telegraph lines and later met exiles of the Russian imperialist government. He spent twenty years lecturing American audiences in support of a Russian revolution. Between these roles, he was a war correspondent for the Associated Press based out of the Corcoran Building, where Joseph Marvin kept his lockbox.

525 T Street NW

(Built 1874)

French S. Evans

This house was also built in 1874 and designed by James McGill. From 1875 to 1887, French S. Evans lived here.

Evans came to Washington as a Methodist reverend. He was associated with Foundry Chapel, Wesley Chapel, Ryland Chapel and McKendree Church, all in Washington. He was later appointed to the Deputy Naval Office of Baltimore at the insistence of President Lincoln himself in 1861.

Evans lived in LeDroit Park in his last few years of life, working at the dead-letter office at the Post Office Department. His job was to help find the recipients of letters that were incorrectly addressed or indecipherable.

W. Scott Smith

W. Scott Smith moved into his house in 1880 and lived here until his death in 1919. He was the Washington correspondent for the *Philadelphia Evening Bulletin* and the *New York Evening Post* and was later editor of two newspapers in New Hampshire. One of the two remaining McGill stables is on the property.

As evidenced by his long tenure in the neighborhood, Smith was invested in LeDroit Park. He was the president of the LeDroit Park Civic Association in the 1880s. This association has been holding community meetings from 1873 to today.

In 1870, he wrote an article about Cuban agents bribing members of Congress with the headline "The Cuban Bond Lobby—Remarkable Discovery—Important, if True." He was brought to the House of Representatives on the charge of slander and was expelled from the reporters' gallery for not naming his sources. A House committee later found that he wasn't malicious but had just reported what he was told and that there "was an excessive rivalry among correspondents…to provide earlier and more startling news than any other."

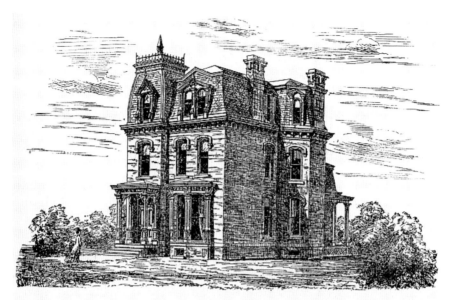

RESIDENCE OF MR. W. SCOTT SMITH, LE DROIT PARK.

Drawing of the house at 525 T Street NW, the home of journalist W. Scott Smith. *James H. McGill's architectural advisor, Printed Materials Collection, DC History Center.*

By the 1930s, the home was being rented out and recorded Black occupants. It is a common thread in oral histories of the neighborhood that Black performers from the Howard Theatre across the street used this as a boardinghouse.

531 T Street NW

(Built 1874)

What are now condos, this was another original McGill duplex home, though there are obvious modern additions on the eastern side.

Early residents of the two houses seemed to come and go quickly, only staying for a year or two. The first resident of the eastern half was Grove K. Gilbert before he moved to the house one block west at the corner of Fourth and T Street NW.

By 1880, Edwin Lamasure lived in this eastern side. At the time, he was a clerk at the U.S. Bureau of Engraving and Printing. He would later become one of the most popular landscape artists at the time.

Just two years before, in 1877–78, the western side was home to John Brisbane Walker.

Walker was a Renaissance man. He had lived in the area before when he attended Georgetown College, but then he left for West Point. He then joined the Chinese army for two years. He made and lost fortunes several times. His time in D.C. in the late 1870s was working with the *Washington Daily Chronicle*. He left that publication after three years to become an alfalfa farmer in Colorado, then bought *Cosmopolitan* magazine (the very same one that exists today).

He sold that to William Randolph Hearst and began to develop much of what is now the Red Rocks area of Colorado. The famous amphitheater was his idea. While spending time in LeDroit Park, he must have become friendly with Amzi Barber, who temporarily moved into this house after Walker left in 1880.

In 1899, Walker and Barber purchased a patent for a steam engine from the Stanley brothers. The Locomobile Company, as Walker and Barber called it, lasted two weeks as a partnership. Walker continued with the Mobile Company of America, which operated for only four years, while Barber's Locomobile continued under the direction of his son-in-law.

A 1900 steam Locomobile. *Grogan Photo Company, Library of Congress.*

4

U Street NW
(Spruce Street)

U Street NW is often associated with the Shaw neighborhood and its "Black Broadway." This is where Pearl Bailey, Marvin Gaye and Duke Ellington are remembered. U Street crosses D.C. from Eighteenth Street NW east to the tracks north of Union Station at Fifth Street NE. However, it does not run continuously and can be found in broken segments. The LeDroit Park section runs only from Sixth Street NW to Third Street NW, where the road dead-ends at the Slowe Apartments. This stretch was originally called Spruce Street.

518 U STREET NW, GEORGE WILLIAM ADAMS

(Built 1890)

George William Adams lived here in the 1920–40s. A Washington, D.C. native, Adams attended M Street / Dunbar High School. He then attended Dartmouth College and later Howard University to receive his medical degree. Dr. Adams joined the Medical Reserve Corps in World War I.

When he returned from the war, he became among the first group of eleven interns at Freedmen's Hospital. He was offered a postgraduate study at Harvard on the Rosenwald Fellowship. Adams was one of the first Black physicians offered this fellowship. He returned to Howard as a pathologist and taught biochemistry and clinical pathology at the medical school.

Dr. Adams was also an avid golfer. He was a founder of the United Golfers Association (UGA). This was a group of Black professional golfers that organized tournaments at the time of segregation. The UGA ended when the Professional Golfers' Association (PGA) repealed the clause allowing only white members.

This house was built by Charles Banes, the Howardtown developer who started the Fence Wars.

512 U STREET NW, WILLIS RICHARDSON

(Built 1901)

Willis Richardson grew up in Washington, D.C., and attended M Street / Dunbar High School. It is here that his teacher Mary Burrill (partner of Lucy Diggs Slowe) encouraged his playwriting.

Richardson was offered a scholarship to attend Howard, but he needed to work to support his family. Instead, he spent most of his life working at the U.S. Bureau of Engraving and Printing. Richardson did not give up his writing. His work *The Chip Woman's Fortune* was the first play by a Black playwright to appear on Broadway. Here he shared a bill with William Shakespeare and Oscar Wilde.

He wrote nearly fifty works and had a number of productions performed, often in places where he was the first Black dramatist. Even in his time, Richardson was considered a "pioneer playwright" and won numerous awards for his plays. He also compiled anthologies. One was at the request of Carter G. Woodson, D.C. resident and the father of "Black History Month," who wanted more educational sources of Black history. It was a school collection that did not include any folk plays written in dialect, as that was considered "inappropriate." Richardson also wrote a collection, *Negro History in Thirteen Plays*, with fellow LeDroit Park resident May Miller.

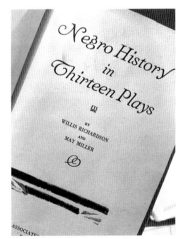

Negro History in Thirteen Plays, anthology by Willis Richardson and May Miller, both LeDroit Park / Howardtown residents. *Author's collection.*

This apartment complex was built in 1901. Richardson lived here with his wife in 1914, when it was called "The Montgomery." Shortly after, he moved farther west down U Street to live just off "Black Broadway."

507 U Street NW, Lawrence Guyot

(Built 1895)

Lawrence Guyot lived here from the 1990s to the early 2000s. Guyot grew up in the "least Mississippi part of Mississippi," where he did not face the same racial segregation and discrimination as seen in the rest of the state. After hearing civil rights activist Medgar Evers speak about other parts of Mississippi, Guyot vowed to do what he could to fight segregation. He joined the Student Nonviolent Coordinating Committee (SNCC) while in college in Mississippi, and there he met other students involved in activism, including Marion Berry. He worked with SNCC and the Mississippi Democratic Freedom Party in the 1960s. As he registered Black voters in Mississippi, he was jailed and beaten, but he returned to register more voters when he was released. The 1965 Voting Rights Act was passed thanks in part to Guyot's efforts.

He moved to Washington, D.C., in 1972 and worked on the election campaign of his friend Marion Barry. Barry became the second mayor of Washington D.C., after LeDroit Park resident Walter Washington. Guyot continued in politics and served as the Advisory Neighborhood Commissioner for LeDroit Park.

Guyot died in 2012, but not before casting his vote to reelect the first Black president.

400 Block of U Street NW

This next block of U Street NW between Fifth and Fourth Streets NW may be the only street of its kind in the United States. All of the homes here are original McGill homes, built in the early 1870s and mostly in the Italian Villa style. All the homes on the south side of the street are double homes, as are most of the ones on the north. They are much more modest than the homes built along T Street NW and Third Street NW.

The 400 Block of U Street NW, original McGill architecture. *Author's collection.*

419 U Street NW (Built 1876)

E.B. Barnum

The corner house was built in 1876 for clothier Ezra B. Barnum by James McGill. Barnum lived here for a few years before moving to another house McGill built for him that is still standing, on Julia Cooper Circle at 1883 Third Street NW.

While living in this house, Barnum was selected to serve on the grand jury for the Guiteau trial. In 1881, Charles Guiteau shot President James A. Garfield. The president died two months later, a result of infections from the wound. Guiteau was arrested, and the grand jury indicted him for murder.

Howard L. Prince

Howard Prince and his family moved in by 1884, having lived just a few doors down at 405 U Street NW in 1880.

Prince worked at first as a clerk in the Police Court of the District of Columbia and later as the librarian of the U.S. Patent Office. Prior to living in D.C., he served as a captain in the Twentieth Maine Volunteer Infantry. He was at the Battle of Gettysburg and was chosen to give a speech at the dedication of the Twentieth Maine Monument at that battlefield. In his speech, he pointed out that he only transported shoes with the help of a mule to the survivors of the battle and that, while he could hear the guns of Gettysburg, he was at a distance.

As the neighborhood changed, so did the occupants of this house. By 1910, this was home to the Brown family. Hiram and Susie Brown were a working-class Black couple. When they moved here, she worked as a printer's assistant at the Bureau of Engraving and Printing, and he was a tonsorial artists (a fancy term for barber). By 1920, Susie was still at the bureau, but Hiram was an elevator foreman at the Post Office Department. They owned the house, free of a mortgage, in 1920.

OSCAR AND JESSIE DE PRIEST

In 1929, Oscar and Jessie De Priest moved into the home. Oscar Stanton De Priest was the first Black congressman elected in the twentieth century and the first ever elected from outside the South. There had not been a Black congressman in the previous twenty-eight years. De Priest had been a politician in Chicago, focusing on the increasing Black population of a city known for its machine politics. He and Jessie lived in this house for his three terms in Congress, during which he was the only Black congressman.

Oscar Stanton De Priest, the first black member of Congress from a northern state, and his wife, Jessie, in 1929. *International Newsreel.*

While he represented the South Side of Chicago, in a way he worked for all of Black America, though with limited success. It was his amendment to the Civilian Conservation Corps that prevented discrimination on race, even if it was not widely enforced.

When Oscar and Jessie arrived in the city, there was a moment of scandal. Or it was an uneventful political tradition. It all depends on who you ask. Tradition was that the First Lady would invite the wives of congressmen to tea at the White House. Jessie De Priest was invited, but the invitation was hand delivered at the last minute, in secrecy, and the guest list was curated from those whose racial views would be amenable to her presence. After the event, many of the southern media and representatives were appalled, while much of the Black population celebrated. For her part, Jessie De Priest found the whole thing pleasant and uneventful.

414 U Street NW

(Built 1876)

Charles Ruoff

Charles Ruoff moved into this house by 1878. As a hatter and farrier, he was best known for providing masonic and military regalia. His firm, Ruoff and Willet, operated out of a storefront on Pennsylvania Avenue NW. It provided gloves, caps and capes for the Treasury Department and badges for the inauguration. The family lived here at least until 1903.

Dr. Harriet Riggs

Shortly after, Harriet Riggs moved in but only for a few years, before she moved to 418 T Street NW. She lived on T Street until her death at the age of 101 in 1956. Harriet was born in Maine to Canadian parents. She attended Howard University, where she earned a medical degree. But as a Black woman in 1901, she did not practice. Dr. Riggs taught at M Street / Dunbar High School for forty years, where she was head of the English and history departments.

Dr. Clara Smyth Taliaferro

When Dr. Riggs left for T Street NW, Clara Smyth moved in. Her father was John H. Smyth, an ambassador to Liberia in the 1880s. Clara had attended schools in D.C., graduating with a doctor of pharmacy degree in 1904. She was one of the few early Black female pharmacists and owned her own drugstore in D.C. in 1910.

Dr. Taliaferro, as she was known after her marriage in 1917, was active in the women's movement and founded the Tuesday Evening Club of Social Workers, which still exists today. The club aims to meet the social needs of Black youth. Dr. Ionia Whippier of Florida Avenue NW was also a member.

413 U Street NW, Warren Choate

(Built 1876)

Warren Choate and family moved here in 1878. When they arrived, he worked as the secretary at the YMCA. Later that year, Choate was hired by the National Capitol Telephone Company. Alexander Graham Bell had invented the telephone just a few years earlier. While the telephone wasn't invented in D.C., Bell was associated with this city. He lived here for much of his adult life and opened the Volta Bureau and Bell Experimental School in D.C.

George Maynard, who owned an electrical supply store south of LeDroit Park on Sixth Street NW, arranged an exclusive license to use Bell telephones in Washington, D.C. He hired Choate in 1878 to canvas the city to find subscribers. Choate was paid seventy-five dollars a month for this job. The goal was to get at least fifty subscribers before Maynard could open a telephone exchange in the city. Choate aimed high and went to the White House, only to be told that the president was not in.

It did not take long for him to reach his goal. The first telephone exchange opened in Washington, D.C., in 1878 with at least fifty subscribers. These included Bell, Bell's father-in-law, the State Department, the Treasury Department, the Willard Hotel and the White House, among others. A few years later, the main exchange had thirty-five operators working under Choate's supervision. He left LeDroit Park and the telephone company in 1887.

406 U Street NW, Garnet C. Wilkinson

(Built 1876)

As a child, Garnet C. Wilkinson attended Birney Elementary in Southeast D.C., named after James Birney, the father of Le Droit founding resident William Birney. Wilkinson's family moved to this house, and he would remain here throughout his life. Wilkinson dedicated his life to the education of Black youth in D.C. as superintendent of "Colored" schools for thirty years.

He had attended M Street / Dunbar High School himself before returning as a teacher and then principal. He was the highest-ranking figure in the school system for Black Washingtonians, though he did answer to the overall superintendent. Under his leadership, the D.C. school system for Black youth continued its national reputation for excellence. His success stories included opening Cardozo High School, which was the only segregated high school in the country to offer business courses to Black students. He focused on vocational studies as well as overall character.

As lauded as he was, Wilkinson was condemned by some. He felt that "separate, but equal" benefited the students under his supervision, and he resisted integration movements. This might have been less about his beliefs in equality and more about the other schools in the system, though. The schools for white students in D.C. were of a much lower caliber. He was active in the NAACP, the Association for the Study of Negro Life and History and the Association of Negro Folk Education.

1936 Fourth Street NW, Ida Gibbs

(Built 1892)

The house at 1936 Fourth Street was the first LeDroit Park home of Mary Church and Robert Terrell. They moved in 1894, just a year after the integration of the neighborhood.

Living with them at this house was Mary's friend Ida Gibbs. Gibbs graduated in the 1884 class at Oberlin University as one of the first Black female graduates, along with Mary Church Terrell and Anna Julia Cooper.

In the late 1890s, all three women were living in LeDroit Park. Over half a century later, the three would meet again at Julia Cooper's T Street NW home. In 1952, the three trailblazing friends, now in their eighties and nineties, met to reminisce. Terrell reminded the reporter covering the story to make sure to include that she was president of the NAACP. "I'm very proud of that," she said. Julia followed up, saying, "And always add that Mrs. Terrell was the youngest in her class."

When the Terrells moved from this house to the one on T Street NW, Gibbs went with them until moving with her sister to Elm Street NW.

Gibbs was one of the early members of the YWCA for Black women in 1905. It was the same YWCA that would later move to LeDroit Park on T Street NW.

1934 Fourth Street NW,
Alice and Paul Laurence Dunbar

(Built 1892)

In 1898, the Dunbars moved in next door at 1934 Fourth Street NW.

Paul Laurence Dunbar was one of the few Black students in his Ohio high school. He started the school newspaper with some friends. Later, one of these friends helped Dunbar self-publish his first book of poems. That friend was Orville Wright, later of Kitty Hawk flight fame.

Dunbar was one of the first Black Americans to be internationally recognized. His poetry was written in both standard and dialect style (the style that Carter G. Woodson didn't want in schools). The first Black musical on Broadway, *In Dahomey*, had lyrics written by Dunbar.

Of his many works, two poems call for special attention. Even if you don't know that you know any of his poems, you likely

Internationally renowned poet Paul Laurence Dunbar, 1905. *Library of Congress.*

have heard the closing line of his poem "Sympathy." It ends with, "I know why the caged bird sings." Poet Maya Angelou used this line as the title of her autobiography.

The second work is a dialect poem from 1906, "Lover's Lane." It was written about the section of U Street just around the corner.

> *Summah night an' sighin' breeze,*
> *'Long de lovah's lane;*
> *Frien'ly, shadder-mekin' trees,*
> *'Long de lovah's lane.*

His wife, Alice Dunbar, wrote of this poem, "The white arc light of the corner lamp, filtering through the arches of the maples on Spruce Street, make for the tender suggestion in 'Lover's Lane,' where the lovers walk side by side under the 'shadder-mekin'" (from "The Poet and His Song" by Alice Dunbar, 1914).

Alice Dunbar was a literary success on her own before meeting Paul. At the age of twenty, she published a collection of short stories, *Violets and Other Tales*. Through her life, she wrote dramas, newspaper columns, speeches, essays, poems, reviews and four novels. Paul had seen one of Alice's works published in 1895 and sent her a letter of introduction. They wrote letters for two years before meeting and got married a year later. Their relationship and time in LeDroit Park were short. The couple moved to LeDroit Park in 1898. Not long after, he was diagnosed with tuberculosis and medicated with alcohol. Despite an abusive relationship, Alice continued working and wrote *The Goodness of St. Rocque, and Other Short Stories* while living here. Paul also continued to write and compile anthologies, but the two separated in 1902 and left LeDroit Park. Paul died in Ohio a few years later, and Alice continued to write and teach in Delaware.

338 U Street NW, Octavius Williams

(Built 1888)

Octavius Williams has the distinction of being the first known Black homeowner in LeDroit Park when his family moved in in 1893. Williams was a barber at the U.S. Capitol. There has been a barbershop at the Capitol since the mid-1800s. Black barbers trimming the hair of politicians at the turn of the century was not uncommon. In fact, the most popular barber from the 1880s to the 1930s was a Black man named John Sims. Sims had escaped slavery before working in the Capitol. His time as a Capitol barber overlaps with Williams, so it is possible they worked together.

Not long after the Williams family moved in, someone shot through the window into their dining room wall. Williams left the bullet hole in the wall as a reminder. He lived here until he died in 1936. His daughter Vivian and her husband, Dr. H. Leroy Pelham, continued to live here at least until the 1940s.

330 U Street NW, Dolores Kendrick

(Built 1888)

LeDroit Park's artistic legacy is also in its more recent history. Dolores Kendrick grew up in this house at 330 U Street NW. Considered Washington,

D.C.'s "First Lady of Poetry," Kendrick was the poet laurate of the capital city for two decades, from 1999 until her death in 2017.

She lived in this house with her mother and uncle, who was an usher at a theater, perhaps nearby Howard Theatre. Her mother, Josephine Kendrick, was a musician who cowrote "My Heart Beats for You," sung by Billy Eckstine.

Kendrick's most notable work, *The Women of Plums: Poems in the Voices of Slave Women*, tells the stories of thirty-four enslaved women from the Middle Passage to the Civil War. While a student at M Street / Dunbar High School, she was told her prose was too flowery. She became one of the most influential poets in D.C., not only due to her work, but also due to her insistence on cultivating youth in artistic pursuits and insisting that artists be paid.

She accepted the title of poet laureate only on the condition that she was be given an office so that she could organize festivals, awards and programs for young artists. You can spot her poetry on the walls of the NoMa metro station and the downtown restaurant Zaytinya.

319–25 U Street NW

(Demolished)

This section of U Street has been demolished, and new row houses were built in the 1990s. The new homes were built by the nonprofit developer Manna Inc. Manna helps low- and moderate-income persons become homeowners. These new units were built in keeping with the designs of the historic row houses in the neighborhood.

The structure at 325 U Street NW was a detached home, but 319 was a row house, like the one still standing at 317, which was built in the 1890s.

Charles E. Fairman

At 325 U Street NW was the home of Charles E. Fairman. Fairman was the first curator of the Capitol Art collection and an art critic for the *Washington Times*. He was curator at the U.S. Capitol when Adelaide Johnson's *Portrait Monument to Lucretia Mott, Elizabeth Cady Stanton and Susan B. Anthony* was unveiled. He was critical of it, as was most of Congress. It was hidden in a broom closet with its inscription scraped off the day

Charles Fairman photograph entitled *Silence*. Photographic Times: An Illustrated Monthly Magazine Devoted to the Interests of Artistic and Scientific Photography, *1901*.

after it was revealed. Fairman was the one who coined the name, though he suggested *Portrait Memorial to Lucretia Mott, Elizabeth Cady Stanton and Susan B. Anthony*. Johnson changed "memorial" to "monument."

Fairman was an amateur photograph himself. He often hosted expositions in his home here in LeDroit Park. He devoted two of the large rooms in his house for displays entirely of his own work, which thousands of people came to view. His work as always well received, and he was known for landscapes and for using models posing as Greek figures.

The Fairmans lived here from the 1890s until the 1940s, one of the last white families to remain in the neighborhood as the demographics changed.

He would have met his neighbor at 319 (also demolished), Christian Fleetwood.

Christian and Sarah Fleetwood

Fleetwood and his wife, Sarah, moved into the house around 1900 and lived here until 1908. Their house at 319 has been demolished but would have looked like the house next door at number 317.

Christian Fleetwood was born into a free family in Maryland, traveled to Liberia and graduated valedictorian of Lincoln University in Pennsylvania. He helped found the *Lyceum Observer* in Baltimore, one of the first Black newspapers in the South, just before the Civil War.

He enlisted in the U.S. Army in 1863 and was so educated that he was immediately promoted to sergeant major in the Fourth Regiment of USCT. Most of the action he saw was around Richmond and Petersburg, Virginia.

At the Battle of Chaffin's Farm, he led the left flank as it ran toward the Confederate garrison. The flagbearer was shot, but a second man grabbed the flag and continued. This second man was wounded, but before the flag could touch the ground, Fleetwood took hold of it and continued the fight. His unit was forced to retreat, but he carried the flag the entire time. For this action, Fleetwood was one of the first Black recipients of the Medal of Honor. This is the same battle in which Ellery Ford of T Street NW served.

Every officer (again, they were all white) in the Fourth petitioned directly to Secretary of War Edwin Stanton to make Fleetwood an officer, but this was denied.

When he returned to D.C., Fleetwood organized one of the first black National Guard units, for which he was finally promoted to an officer's rank. This unit was the origin of the First Separate Battalion.

Fleetwood's Medal of Honor is currently on display at the Smithsonian Museum of American History. When he died in 1914, the First Separate Battalion performed the military escort. Serving in the First Separate Battalion at the time were James E. Walker and West A. Hamilton, both of whom lived on T Street NW.

Portrait of Medal of Honor recipient Christian Fleetwood, circa 1900. *Library of Congress.*

Sarah Fleetwood was a member of the first graduating class of the Freedmen's Hospital Training School in 1896. Not long after, she became the superintendent of the Training School for Nurses. Sarah was the first Black woman to serve on the city's nurse's examining board. Her great-grandfather was Aaron Burr, vice president of the United States but most remembered for killing Alexander Hamilton in a duel.

The Fleetwoods were active in the social and artistic scene developing in the neighborhood at the turn of the century. They hosted evening salons to discuss music, poetry and art and formed the "Mignonette Club" to put on plays and concerts. They stressed that there would be no refreshments at these evenings—"a decision to ensure the permanency of these entertainments."

The Fleetwoods left LeDroit Park in 1908 and moved farther north in the city.

317 U Street NW, Theresa Brown

(Built 1890)

Theresa Brown moved to LeDroit Park in 1957 from Baltimore and realized that there was something special about this neighborhood. When she arrived, it was no longer at its height of elite residents, but it wasn't so long past that time that remnants weren't still there. With integration, many residents left LeDroit Park, and some of the grander buildings were torn down in favor of multifamily units. She spearheaded the efforts to save the neighborhood and preserve its history. The LeDroit Park Preservation Society that she formed would write the application for the neighborhood to become a historic district. In 1974, the National Register of Historic Places approved the application. LeDroit was the third historic district in D.C., following Georgetown and Anacostia.

Brown also preserved the Otis O. Howard House on the campus of Howard University and the Whitelaw Hotel off U Street NW, and she helped move the D.C. City Museum into the old Carnegie library—what is now an Apple store, though the D.C. History Center is still located in the building.

She was joined in the pursuit of preservation by Lauretta Jackson of 410 U Street NW. Jackson had lived in that home since the 1940s and worked with Brown as the secretary of the LeDroit Park Civic Association. It is thanks to Brown and Jackson that many of the homes discussed in this book are standing today.

1922 Third Street NW, J. Joseph Albright

(Built 1874)

Note the carriage house that is across the street. It is the other remaining McGill stable and has been converted into a loft apartment. The carriage house belongs to the house on the corner of U Street NW and Third Street NW.

This was an early McGill house, built in 1874 for J. Joseph Albright. Albright was a business partner of both Amzi Barber and Andrew Langdon. The three were also brothers-in-law.

Prior to moving to D.C., Albright and Langdon were partnered in a coal business. When Albright moved in 1873, he, Langdon and Barber all lived in LeDroit Park. Though eventually Barber moved on to become "Asphalt King" and Albright moved to steel, Albright continued to operate a coal business out of the LeDroit Building in downtown D.C. until the early 1900s.

The LeDroit Building, on F Street NW, was designed by James McGill and held the offices of Barber and McGill, as well William H. Boyd, who published *Boyd's Directory*, which informed most of this book. In recent years, the LeDroit Building was home to the International Spy Museum until 2019.

Left: Original McGill carriage house, now a private residence. *Author's collection.*

Right: Original McGill home at the corner of Third Street and U Street NW. *Author's collection.*

Albright also invested in Barber's failed Locomobile company. Most of his later life and philanthropical work centered on Buffalo, New York, where he lived after his few years in LeDroit Park.

1938 Third Street NW, Edward Brooke

(Built 1890)

Edward Brooke was born in this house at 1938 Third Street NW in 1919. Like most of the residents of LeDroit Park at the time, he attended M Street / Dunbar High School and Howard University. His father, another graduate of Howard Law, was a lawyer for the Veterans Administration.

When World War II broke out and Brooke enlisted, he used what he had learned from his father to defend enlisted men in military court.

After the war, he officially studied law at Boston University Law School and centered his political career in Massachusetts. He served as chairman of the Boston Finance Commission, attorney general of Massachusetts (the first elected Black attorney general of any state) and then senator for the Commonwealth of Massachusetts.

He was the first Black man popularly elected to the U.S. Senate, this happening in 1966. Previous Black senators had been appointed or elected by a state legislature.

1955 Third Street NW, Duke Ellington

(Built 1890)

Just across the street, possibly still living there to witness the birth of future senator Edward Brooke, was a newlywed couple, Duke and Edna Ellington.

Duke Ellington's time in Washington, D.C., is mostly associated with the western part of U Street NW known as "Black Broadway," but he had lived in LeDroit Park before as a child. In 1906, he lived at 420 Elm Street NW, when he was seven years old.

Biographies say that Ellington began piano lessons at the same age, so it may be that he started lessons while at that Elm Street house. Though his mother played and taught him at an early age, formal piano lessons began with Marietta Clinkscales—an apt name for a piano teacher. She lived south of LeDroit Park in Judiciary Square, an easy streetcar ride on the Metropolitan line.

Duke Ellington's first job was selling peanuts at Washington Senators games at Griffith Stadium, which straddled the neighborhood boundary between LeDroit Park and Shaw.

Just south of Griffith Stadium at the northeast corner of Georgia Avenue NW and Seventh Street NW was a soda shop called Poodle Dog Café. It was here that Duke Ellington worked in the 1920s as a soda jerk. The café advertised live music. The story goes that the pianist would sometimes fall off his stool, drunk, and the young Ellington would jump in to play. He wrote a tune called "Poodle Dog Rag," later retitled "Soda Fountain Rag."

May Miller was a playwright who lived nearby and worked with LeDroit Park resident Willis Richardson on an anthology on Black playwrights. One of her early plays, *Scratches*, from 1929, took place in the "Poodle Dog Pool Parlor" in LeDroit Park. Writings about the café regarding Ellington always call it a soda shop, but in 1922, it was raided for gambling, so it may have some seedy undertones. The building has long since been demolished, as has

Griffith Stadium. Only this house and the one at 420 Elm Street NW remain as sites related to Duke Ellington's time in LeDroit Park.

After Duke married Edna in 1918, they moved into this house at 1955 Third Street NW but lived here for only one year. Much of the rest of Duke's life was spent closer to U Street's musical center or in Harlem.

5

Elm Street NW

Elm Street kept its original name when the neighborhood adopted the city's naming system. Technically, though, Elm wasn't its original name. For the first years of LeDroit Park, it was also called McClelland Street. It was at the northern boundary of the original suburb, and the fence would have been along the north side of Elm. From Fifth Street NW to Fourth Street NW, there were no houses on the north side of the road. Moving east, at the northern terminus of Third Street NW, the development extended north slightly, so there were some houses along Third Street NW past Elm.

Most of the houses with Elm addresses today were built after the fenced-in days of LeDroit Park. There had been some detached homes, likely designed by McGill. Most of them are long gone, though a few remain on Elm Street.

These homes were smaller than the grand residences on T Street NW. From the beginning, this northern section of LeDroit Park was home to working-class residents. The homes were important to someone, but not to the historical record, and there isn't much written about them.

Residents on Elm Street through the turn of the twentieth century were mostly laborers, dressmakers, drivers and servants. However, like the rest of the neighborhood, there were clerks for various departments of the federal governments and, of course, someone associated with the U.S. Geological Survey.

In the 1890s, Frederick C. Ohm lived on Elm. He worked at the USGS. Ohm was born in Denmark; his father was the court photographer for the

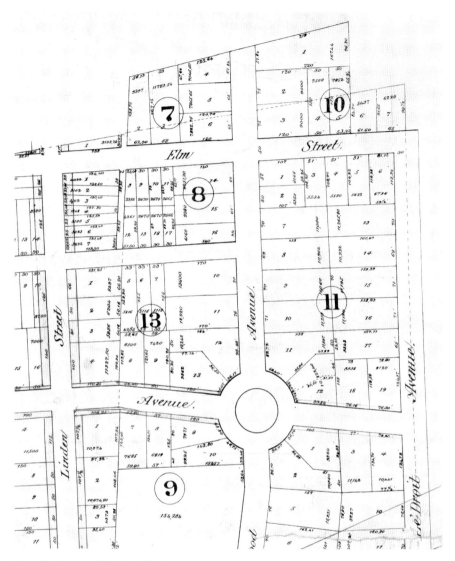

Late 1880s map of LeDroit Park as recorded in the Surveyor's Office, A.L. Barber & Company. *Library of Congress.*

king of Denmark. Frederick was considered one of the foremost section makers in petrographic analysis in the United States during his time at the survey. A section maker makes thin sections of rock for analysis and research.

Possible McGill Homes

The house at 1946 Third Street NW was one of the first houses built in the neighborhood, erected in 1874. At that time, the northern side of the house bordered Elm Street NW.

The open lots that had been yards of the larger mansions were built on when the neighborhood started growing. The house that is now on the corner of Third Street NW and Elm Street NW was built in 1907.

The house on Elm Street NW at number 216 stands out as another original—or, rather, it stands back. It is significantly more set back than the newer houses around it. These newer homes were built in 1908. It cannot be definitively called a McGill home, but it was built in the 1880s as a detached house. Most subsequent architects for the neighborhood designed row houses.

327 Elm Street NW

(Built 1896)

When Harriet Gibbs first moved to Washington, D.C., in 1900, she lived here on Elm Street NW. Her sister Ida Gibbs had already been living in LeDroit Park with the Terrells.

Harriet offered her services as a music teacher from their home. The sisters were born in Canada to a wealthy and successful Black family that immigrated to Canada after the California Gold Rush. Their father, Mifflin Gibbs, was a lawyer and politician. He was the first Black judge elected in the United States, in 1873. He was in Little Rock, Arkansas, at the time.

Harriet graduated from the Oberlin Conservatory for Music, the first Black woman to do so. When she arrived in D.C., she taught music at M Street / Dunbar High School. Her father purchased a property on the 900 block of T Street NW, not far from LeDroit Park. She opened the Washington Conservatory of Music and School of Expression here in 1903. This was a private music school, and it operated until 1960, making it the longest-operating music school for Black students.

In 1913, Harriet was one of a few Black women to march in the Women's Suffrage Parade, along with Mary Church Terrell.

THE CRISIS ADVERTISER   49

Established 1876   Telephone 1708 Harlem

The MANDO

Mozart Conservatory of Music, Inc.
2105 Madison Avenue   New York

Branches of Instruction:
Violin, Violoncello, Harmony, Ensemble Playing,
Chamber Music. The course of instruction adopted
throughout all departments is thorough and pre-
cisely the same as taught in the leading conserva-
tories in this city and in Europe.
The Conservatory Sextette and Concert Orchestra,
Mrs. Eliza Mando, Conductor, is open for engage-
ments for concerts and all occasions where superior
music is required. Terms reasonable.
For further information address
MRS. ELIZA MANDO, Director

HARRIET GIBBS-MARSHALL, President   LOUIS G. GREGORY, Financial Secretary
HARRY A. WILLIAMS, Vice-President   GREGORIA A. FRASER, Recording Secretary

The Washington Conservatory of Music and School of Expression

Piano, Violin, Wind Instruments, Piano Tuning, Vocal Expression, History of
Music Theory and Modern Languages

The first and only Mission Music School founded and controlled by Negroes
in America.

Many scholarships awarded. Talented students never turned away unaided.

902 T Street, N. W.   WASHINGTON, D. C.

Mrs. DAISY TAPLEY

Teacher of voice and piano, will take a limited
number of pupils during the summer months.
Choruses trained, soloists coached. Engagements
for concerts solicited. For terms and appointments
address the studio:

172 West 133d Street   NEW YORK

MME. FANNIE BELLE DE KNIGHT

Dramatic and Dialect Reader. Engagements so-
licited. Students given special training in the
Delsarte Method. Instruction also given in Dialect,
English Grammar and Rhetoric.

Terms Reasonable.
Telephone Morningside 9045

Studio: 231 W. 134th St.   New York City

HARMONY AND COMPOSITION

TAUGHT BY MAIL
Interesting and Comprehensive Course.
Small monthly payments.
Address
J. HILLARY TAYLOR
Director The Success Piano School.
43 O Street, N. E.   Washington, D. C.
Bell Telephone.

Telephone Connection

"DEACON" JOHNSON
(That Cheerful Entertainer)
Leader, Mandolin and Second Tenor with
THE "DEACON" JOHNSON QUARTET
Montreal   New York   Philadelphia
Permanent Address:
Times Sq. Sta., Box 317, New York City

Mme. MARIE JACKSON STUART'S

School of Expression, Music and Dramatic Art

A thorough, well-defined course of instruction,
designed to give the student a comprehensive grasp
of each subject in the shortest time. Terms
reasonable.

Dramas staged. Amateurs trained. Plays revised.
ADDRESS
33 West 131st Street   New York

Miss MINNIE BROWN

SOPRANO

May be engaged for commencements, concerts and
recitals. For terms address:

172 West 133d Street   NEW YORK
Care of Tapley Studio

TURN YOUR SPARE MOMENTS INTO CASH

The increasing sales of THE CRISIS have so
far exceeded our expectations that we must
have more representatives to look after our
interests in each locality.

The work is dignified as well as profitable,
and will not interfere with your present
occupation. Address

Sales Manager of THE CRISIS

26 Vesey Street   New York

Mention THE CRISIS.

Advertisement for Harriet Gibbs's Washington Conservatory of Music and School of Expression. The Crisis, *1912*.

309 Elm Street NW

(Built 1890)

The earliest recorded resident of this house was William H.H. Warman. He lived here as early as 1879 while working as a clerk in the Bureau of Pensions. He served in the American Civil War with the Thirty-First New Jersey Regiment.

Later, in the early 1900s, William Pemberton Richards lived here. Richards oversaw condemnations of land and street extension from 1895 to 1905. Then he was a surveyor for the District of Columbia from 1905 to 1908. In this role, he determined property boundaries within the city. For the next twenty years, he was the city assessor, determining the value of individual properties.

His tenure of working on street extensions corresponds with the extension of Rhode Island Avenue NW through LeDroit Park.

Park at LeDroit

The Park at LeDroit is the site of the old Gage-Eckington School. The elementary school, built in the 1970s, was closed in 2008. The Gage-Eckington School was named after the two previous elementary schools in the area, Gage Elementary and Eckington Elementary. Gage was around the corner on Second Street NW. Both buildings were erected as schools for white students, even though the neighborhoods were mostly Black.

When the Gage-Eckington Elementary School closed, there was a proposal for the empty building to be renovated into a city government building for D.C. This proposal failed once it was realized that there was no parking. Instead, the building was razed, and this neighborhood park was created.

Note the mural on the side of 239 Elm Street NW. It was painted in 2008, before the elementary school was demolished. Titled *This Is How We Live*, it was painted by muralist Garin Baker. Baker is a New York artist who has completed public art murals in the United States and abroad. This piece focuses on the Black history of LeDroit Park. The mural shows the street scene at the LeDroit Park archway at the intersection of Sixth Street NW and Florida Avenue looking east along T Street. You can see insets of the U.S. Capitol building. There are views of the Capitol from some of the higher apartment buildings around Fifth Street and Florida Avenue NW. Though the mural shows the view looking down Pennsylvania Avenue NW downtown. You can also see Howard University's Founders Library, with its distinctive clock tower. This view can be seen by looking north on Fifth Street NW in LeDroit Park.

Before it was a park, it was the elementary school. And before it was the school, it was Third Street NW. The road extended one block north, just across Oakdale Place, and on either side were homes.

There were a pair of apartment buildings called the Linden and the Harewood. These names pay homage to two of the original street names in LeDroit Park. Harewood became Third Street NW where the apartment building stood. The Harewood and The Linden were on the corner of Third Street NW and Oakdale, about where the southern part of the Common Good City Farm is today. They were owned by Charles Banes, one of the Howardtown developers who started the Fence Wars.

In 1901, the apartments were advertised in a weekly publication called the *Colored American*. This is only ten years after the fences were torn down, so the transition from exclusive white to Black is evident. In the ad, Banes says:

> *Le Droit Park has become a pleasant part of Washington in which to reside and these beautiful flats are a happy addition to the residences there.… Colored people with first class reference who desire a beautiful part of the city in which to live, and at the same time occupy comfortable and improved apartments without renting a whole house, and paying high rent, can find a happy medium in these flats.*

Just south of the Harewood and Linden apartments was an original McGill home. Today, it's the southwest corner of the Park at LeDroit, the open grassy area beyond the bike rack. Joseph Maddren lived here by at least 1879.

Though he was born in England, Maddren lived in Brooklyn, New York prior to LeDroit Park. He was naturalized in 1856. He and his son, also named Joseph, were bookbinders with the U.S. Government Printing Office in New York City and in D.C. Joseph Maddren must have been good, as he was one of the highest-paid bookbinders in 1885 in D.C.

211 Elm Street NW, Carver Apartments

(Built 1942)

This is the companion building to the Slowe Apartments. But this was built for the Black men working for the federal government during World War II. Like Slowe, it was built in 1942 and designed by architect Hilyard Robinson.

Both Slowe Hall and Carver Hall were built by the Defense Homes Corporation. This entity was incorporated in 1940 to help create housing for war industry workers. It existed until 1942, but the buildings were not transferred in 1948.

There were two bills in Congress to address the fate of these two dormitories. One proposed that they be transferred to Howard University. The other proposed that they both be transferred to the Booker T. Washington Birthplace Memorial. The Booker T. Washington proposal was that the two buildings be used for a National Institute of Industrial Training for Negro Youth. Its purpose was to offer education to Black men who served in World War II but were not eligible to use the GI Bill to attend college because they had not attended high school. Many school districts in the United States did not have approved secondary schools for Black youth in the 1940s.

By 1948, many of the rooms in Carver Hall were already occupied by veterans who were attending Howard University. The decision was made to transfer the properties to Howard. The congressional committee stated that the Booker T. Washington Birthplace Memorial was a private institution with no history of education and whose proposal focused only on industrial training. Also, Howard University was just down the street.

Just like Slowe Hall, it was redeveloped in the 2010s as an apartment complex.

Before Carver Hall was built in 1940s, there were single-family homes here. In the 1890s, Second Street NW ended here at Elm Street and did not continue north.

Three detached homes stood where Carver Hall was built. At least two of them were erected in the 1880s, likely by James McGill.

At the home that used to stand on the corner, some fifteen years after Campbell Hospital closed, its commissary sergeant moved back to the neighborhood that had replaced the hospital. Thomas R. Senior moved to this house in LeDroit Park. At this point, he was working as a clerk at the U.S. Department of Agriculture. He was one of the first residents to live on Elm Street NW when he moved in in 1879.

2035 Second Street NW, Nathanial Parker Gage School

(Built 1904)

Another historic building turned condo, the Gage School was built in 1904. When the structure was renovated in 2008, it had been vacant for nearly thirty years. Though considered a Bloomingdale landmark today, at the time it was built, it was referred to as "the new school in LeDroit Park."

The public school was named for Nathanial Parker Gage, a supervising principal in the D.C. school system in the 1870s through the 1890s. There is a very specific report from the 1880s that provides several details about Gage. It says that he was five feet, ten inches tall, 155 pounds with black hair, a full beard and a dark complexion. The report states that as of 1884 he was a bachelor and "there are symptoms of it becoming chronic."

The school was built at a time when the demographics of LeDroit Park were changing. However, it remained a school for white children only from 1904 until desegregation in the 1950s. The school closed entirely in the 1970s.

1948 Second Street NW, Josephine Carroll Smith

(Built 1918)

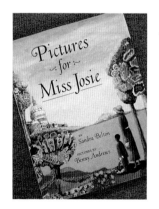

Sandra Belton's *Letters for Miss Josie* children's book about Josephine C. Carroll. *Author's collection.*

Josephine Carroll Smith was an educator involved in the D.C. public school system from 1916 to 1955. Her parents were former enslaved persons who helped found the Shiloh Baptist Church in the nearby Shaw neighborhood. Smith had attended M Street / Dunbar High School, Miner's Teachers College and Howard University. She was a teacher, principal, division director and director of elementary education.

After integration, she was the first director of elementary education across the entire D.C. school system. She drew the boundaries that ended segregation in the city.

Smith's dedication to her students is memorialized in the book *Pictures for Miss Josie* by Sandra Belton. Smith died in 1997 at the age of 103.

Her house was on the border of LeDroit Park and Bloomingdale here on Second Street NW. Though she was on the Bloomingdale Civic Association rather than the LeDroit Park one, Smith would have been known by and was friendly with the many residents in LeDroit during the 1930s and '40s.

PART III

ENVIRONS

THE HISTORIC DISTRICT OF LeDroit Park comprises only a few square blocks. But some of the surrounding areas are pivotal to its history, even if not technically within the LeDroit Park boundary.

6

Howard University

Most prominent among the nearby areas that affected LeDroit Park is Howard University. The two are very much entwined from the beginning of the neighborhood's history until today.

At the end of the Civil War, there was a discussion at the First Congregationalist Church in Washington, D.C., on providing educational opportunities to the newly freed Black residents of Washington. The increase in the Black population of the city in the late 1860s was drastic. The discussion started with a theological school for Black clergymen and quickly developed into a university for all.

Howard University was charted in 1867 by Congress and is still a private university but with an endowment from Congress. The founding members named the school after Otis Oliver Howard, commissioner of the Freedmen's Bureau at the time. He was one of the ten-person group that started the movement for the school. He objected to the naming and was told to imagine that it was named for British philanthropist John Howard rather than himself.

John A. Smith had been a slave owner and owned the large parcel of land north of McClelland, Gilman and Moore. When he was approached about selling a portion of his land, he said that all of it should be purchased or none of it. With this, they purchased the entire plot, and Howard owned more land than it needed, but it continued to expand. In 1870, it also purchased the triangular Miller tract along Boundary Street. On the board of trustees by this time was Amzi Barber.

Chemistry laboratory at Howard University, Washington, D.C., circa 1900. *Library of Congress.*

Amzi Barber's father was a Congregationalist pastor, so while Amzi did not follow that career path, it makes sense that he came to teach at a school founded by Congregationalists. He was persuaded by General O.O. Howard, then president of the nascent school, to became principal of the Normal School at Howard.

Shortly after purchasing the Miller tract, Howard sold the land to the developers of LeDroit Park. In a way, Barber sold the land to himself.

Howard continued to grow in physical size, student body and reputation. It has always been open to students of any religion, gender or race and has offered a variety of degrees. Since it was open to all races at a time when this was uncommon, it became a stalwart in the education of Black Washingtonians. Students of M Street / Dunbar High School became students at Howard and then became teachers at M Street / Dunbar High. Many students continued their educational pursuits at Ivy League schools, only to find that they were not welcome to teach or research at those same schools. They returned to Howard and to LeDroit Park.

Howard's connection to LeDroit Park continued long past integration. The school began to purchase back many of the lots in LeDroit Park in the mid-twentieth century. After World War II, the university used Slowe Hall as a dormitory for students.

The plan had been to raze the old homes and extend the Howard University Hospital. This was stopped when LeDroit Park became a historic district. Restoring or even maintaining the homes it purchased in the neighborhood was a low priority until recently. Through efforts of LeDroit Park residents in the 1990s, the school began to improve and sell homes to Howard staff and faculty and city employees. Howard still owns the historic homes of Bennetta and Walter Washington and Mary Church and Robert Terrell. Both buildings are slowly being restored.

7

Howardtown

Outside the bounds of the original fences of LeDroit Park are areas that over the years have switched between being part of Howardtown and LeDroit Park. Here were the homes of influential Americans who would have been frequent figures as it became a prosperous Black neighborhood.

At Fourth Street NW and Bryant Street NW, about three blocks north of LeDroit Park, in what is now a Howard University parking lot, was the home of Kelly Miller. His family lived here from 1897 until his death in 1939. Miller taught at Howard University and created its sociology department. As a sociologist, Miller fought the belief that race was the reason behind problems in Black communities.

He was friends with LeDroit Park residents Paul Laurence Dunbar and Langston Hughes. Growing up influenced by these figures, his daughter May Miller became an accomplished poet and playwright. She coauthored the anthology *Negro History in Thirteen Plays* with Willis Richardson and compared the neighborhood to Harlem, saying it didn't need a renaissance.

Just around the corner, the stretch of W Street NW around Howard University was originally called Pomeroy Street. Growing up on the 300 block of Pomeroy were Benjamin O. Davis Sr. and Eva Dykes.

They were not contemporaries. When Davis lived here in the 1880s, this was open farmland, and his family kept cows. Benjamin O. Davis Sr was the first Black general in the U.S. Army.

By the time Eva Dykes was born in 1893, the area had become more developed. Her mother was a dressmaker, and her uncle, with whom they lived along with her grandfather, was a physician. She attended M Street / Dunbar High School and Howard University. Eva continued her studies at Radcliffe College, the sister school to Harvard at a time when the universities were separated by gender. Technically, Eva Dykes was the first Black woman to earn a PhD when she completed requirements in 1921. But she was the third to physically receive her degree, as Radcliffe's graduation ceremonies happened late. Eva returned to D.C. to teach at M Street / Dunbar High and Howard University until the 1940s, though she lived outside of LeDroit Park.

8

M Street / Dunbar High School

Throughout the book, this double name has been used for the school. Dunbar High School can trace its story from the M Street High School, but they were different schools in different locations at different times. The M Street High School was one of the first public high schools for Black students in the United States and had success throughout its existence. However, Dunbar has the name recognition of being the preeminent school for Black students in the early twentieth century. To confer that appreciation to its predecessor, M Street High School, the two names have been listed together each time the school is mentioned, regardless of which name was used during the time being discussed.

When the school was founded in 1870, it was the Preparatory High School for Negro Youth. It would take twenty years of funding from Congress to build a permanent school. This school was built on M Street NW. The school focused on classical education as well as character development. With its incredibly high standards, graduates went on to Harvard, Yale, Dartmouth and Brown. Due to its reputation, Black families would move to Washington, D.C., so that their children could attend.

In addition to academics, the school was known for the Cadet Corps. The Cadet Corps was found in most area high schools in the first half of the twentieth century. The first Cadet Corps for Black students was created at M Street High School in 1888 by Christian Fleetwood. Its annual drill competition was held at Griffith Stadium.

Photograph of "M Street High School Cadets" by Hamilton Sutton Smith, from between 1895 and 1900. *Museum of African American History, Boston and Nantucket.*

In 1916, the school was moved to a new location and named Dunbar in honor of Paul Laurence Dunbar. In a time when high schools were divided between academic and vocational, Dunbar focused on academics. Most of the faculty members held master's degrees and PhDs, and the school was sending 80 percent of its graduates to college. This was before integration. Originally, Dunbar accepted only the brightest students from anywhere in the city who could meet the entrance exams. After integration, it became a neighborhood school, and the student body, while remaining mostly Black, was no longer as academically driven as those in previous eras.

Because of the school's high standard of academic excellence in the early 1900s and LeDroit Park's level of intellectualism, the two are closely related. Most of the residents of LeDroit Park after it became predominately Black had attended M Street / Dunbar High School. Many of them would teach there as well. Julia Cooper, Mary Church and Robert Terrell, Christian Fleetwood and Ernest Everett Just are a few of the distinguished faculty who lived in LeDroit Park.

9

Griffith Stadium

Unlike M Street / Dunbar High School and Howard University, Griffith Stadium was not a part of the everyday lives of many people introduced in the preceding chapters. Though they likely attended some games. But you cannot talk about LeDroit Park without mentioning Griffith Stadium.

The current Howard University Hospital takes up the block that used to be the baseball stadium. It was located just north of LeDroit Park's shortest section next to Georgia Avenue. The baseball stadium's right field ran along Fifth Street NW. Today, there is a marker inside the hospital that shows where the home plate was located.

In 1891, around the time that the streets were being opened and the fences torn down around LeDroit Park, Boundary Field opened. It was named after nearby Boundary Street.

This was home field to the Washington Senators. This name was used for the team that played from 1891 to 1899, and then again from 1904 to 1960. For some years between these eras, they were also called the Washington Nationals. Though there is a Washington Nationals baseball team today, it is not the same franchise. The original Washington Senators became the Minnesota Twins; the Senators that played in D.C. from 1961 to 1972 would become the Texas Rangers. The original Senators from the pre 1960s era were the team that was "first in peace, first in war, last in the American league" and that could never beat those "damn Yankees."

Howard University Hospital, where Griffith Stadium used to stand. *Author's collection.*

This wooden stadium was the birthplace of a great baseball pastime. In April 1910, President William H. Taft threw out the ceremonial first pitch to open the season. Almost every president since has done the same.

The stadium was destroyed in a fire just before the 1911 season. Rather than delay the games, a new steel-and-concrete structure was quickly built. Susie and Hiram Brown, Dr. Clara Taliaferro and Garnet C. Wilkinson, all living just around the corner on the 400 block of U Street, would have heard the laborers working day and night.

The new Nationals Park was completed in time for Opening Day in 1911, and Taft threw the first pitch. The new stadium was very much in the neighborhood. It was surrounded by residences on two sides just beyond the bleachers. Five homeowners along Fifth Street NW across from Elm Street NW refused to sell their homes. Their houses and a large tree in the backyard forced the right-field fence line to bend.

LeDroit Park residents attended games and worked there. Duke Ellington sold hot dogs as one of his early jobs.

For most of their time in D.C., the team was owned by Clark Griffith. The venue was renamed Griffith Stadium in 1923. Apart from the 1920s, when

A 1905 view of the original wooden Boundary Park Stadium, before the new steel-and-concrete Griffith Stadium was erected. The wooden stadium was destroyed by fire in 1911. *Geo. R. Lawrence Co., Library of Congress.*

they won the World Series once and came close a few times, the Washington Senators were a low-ranked team. One of the best players in the game, Walter Johnson, however, spent his entire twenty-one-year career playing for the Senators.

To be fair, this was the pinnacle of all-star baseball. Lou Gehrig, Joe DiMaggio, Hank Greenburg, Babe Ruth and Mickey Mantle all played here—for opposing teams. In 1953, Mantle hit a historic home run at Griffith Stadium. He had debuted for the New York Yankees two days earlier. In the top of the fifth and with Yogi Berra on first, Mantle hit one of the longest recorded home runs in baseball history, 565 feet. It went so far that it landed in the backyard of a family living at 434 Oakdale Place in LeDroit Park. Mantle was the first player in Major League Baseball history to hit a ball out of the park at Griffith Stadium, a feat even Joe DiMaggio did not accomplish. It was called a "tape-measure home run," and the term has been used for especially long-distance home runs ever since.

When the Senators weren't playing at home, the stadium was used by the Homestead Grays, a Negro League team from Pennsylvania. They were good. Fan attendance to Grays games were so high that the team played more than two-thirds of its games in D.C. Cumberland Posey, Smokey Joe Williams, Cool Papa Bell and Josh Gibson were players for the Grays.

Homestead Grays star hitter Josh Gibson would likely have beat Mantle's record of longest home run, possibly more than once. It is said he hit a 580-foot home run out of Yankee Stadium. While Mantle is often credited as the first player to hit a home run out of Griffith Stadium, Gibson did it in 1939. Many of his hits were not measured and were not considered

Aerial photograph of Griffith Stadium in Washington, D.C., 1925. *National Archives*.

Baseball card from 1961, "Mickey Mantle Blasts 565 ft. Home Run." *Author's collection*.

official, since he played in the Negro National League and not for Major League Baseball.

When the Homestead Grays and Washington Senators were not utilizing the field, local sandlot teams played here. The LeDroit Tigers was a local team in the 1920s. They were the champions of the Black semipro teams in Washington, D.C. Jesse "Nip" Winters, the best pitcher in the Eastern Negro League, got his start on the team before he eventually returned to Griffith Stadium as a Homestead Gray.

Sam Lacy also began his career as a LeDroit Tiger. He was a pitcher with a great curveball and was even recruited by white teams—they billed him as an Algonquin Indian. He proved to be a great pitcher but an even better sports reporter. He became the first Black sports journalist to join the Baseball Writers Association of America. His sportswriting career spans the 1920s through Jesse Owens, Joe Louis, Satchel Paige and Jackie Robinson. His final article was filed at the age of ninety-nine from his hospital bed in 2003.

Afterword

LeDroit Park Today

L eDroit Park has had many changes over the past century and a half. It began as a gated, whites-only suburb full of large homes with open lawns. The gates came down, and it became a mostly Black neighborhood for the well-educated and politically minded. The yards were filled in with row houses, and the streets were renamed. The city of Washington expanded around it.

LeDroit Park archway surrounded by eastern redbuds in the spring. *Author's collection*.

But some things didn't change. The tree-lined streets that were a marketing point in 1873 still provide shade to passersby. The flowers in the gardens that led to LeDroit Park's nickname, the "Gardens of Washington, D.C.," still bloom. Each spring, as in decades past, people come to LeDroit Park to see the floral landscape. Hopefully, now there will be some #history along with the #cherryblossoms on social media.

Further Reading

Belton, Sandra. *Pictures for Miss Josie*. New York: HarperCollins, 2003.

Cooper, Anna J. *The Voice of Anna Julia Cooper: Including a Voice from the South and Other Important Essays, Papers, and Letters*. Lanham, MD: Rowman & Littlefield Publishers, 2000.

Dunbar, Paul Laurence, William Dean Howells and Lida Keck Wiggins. *The Life and Works of Paul Laurence Dunbar: Containing His Complete Poetical Works, His Best Short Stories, Numerous Anecdotes and a Complete Biography of the Famous Poet*. Naperville, IL: J.L. Nichols, 1907.

Fidler, Eric. *Left for LeDroit* (blog). www.leftforledroit.com

Handy, Antoinette D. *The International Sweethearts of Rhythm: The Ladies' Jazz Band from Piney Woods Country Life School*. Lanham, MD: Scarecrow Press, 1998.

Hughes, Langston. *The Big Sea*. Czechia: Good Press, 2021.

Malinowski, Shilpi. *Shaw, LeDroit Park & Bloomingdale in Washington, D.C.: An Oral History*. Charleston, SC: The History Press, 2021.

Manning, Kenneth R. *Black Apollo of Science: The Life of Ernest Everett Just*. New York: Oxford University Press, USA, 1985.

Parker, Alison M. *Unceasing Militant: The Life of Mary Church Terrell*. Chapel Hill: University of North Carolina Press, 2020.

Snyder, Brad. *Beyond the Shadow of the Senators*. New York: McGraw-Hill Education, 2004.

Stewart, Alison. *First Class the Legacy of Dunbar, America's First Black Public High School*. Chicago: Chicago Review Press, 2013.

Terrell, Mary Church. *A Colored Woman in a White World.* Boston: G.K. Hall, 1996.

Washington, John E. *They Knew Lincoln.* New York: Oxford University Press, 2018.

Selected Bibliography

Afro-American Bicentennial Corporation. *A Summary Report of Thirty Sites Determined to Be Significant in Illustrating and Commemorating the Role of Black Americans in United States History*. Washington, DC, 1973.

Barber, Amzi Lorenzo. *Le Droit Park Illustrated*. Washington, DC: R. Beresford, printer, 1877.

Benedetto, Robert, Jane Donovan and Kathleen Du Vall. *Historical Dictionary of Washington, D.C.* Lanham, MD: Scarecrow Press, 2003.

Beresford, R, and A.L. Barber and Co. 1875. "Le Droit Advertiser." *Le Droit Advertiser*.

Boyd's Directory of the District of Columbia. United States: W.H. Boyd, 1873–1923.

Burwell, Lilian Thomas. "Reflections on LeDroit Park: Hilda Wilkinson Brown and Her Neighborhood," *Washington History* 3, no. 2 (Fall/Winter, 1991/92).

Carr, Lynch Associates. *LeDroit Park Conserved*. Washington, DC: Department of Housing and Community Development, 1979.

———. *A Program of Neighborhood Conservation for the Anacostia and LeDroit Park Historic Districts: Final Report*. Cambridge, MA: Environmental Design, 1978.

Cobb, W.M. "Simeon Lewis Carson, M.D., 1882–1954." *Journal of the National Medical Association* 46, no. 6 (1954): 414–19.

DeFerrari, John. *Historic Restaurants of Washington D.C: Capital Eats*. Charleston, SC: The History Press, 2013.

Downing, Andrew Jackson. *The Architecture of Country Houses: Including Designs for Cottages, Farm Houses, and Villas, with Remarks on Interiors, Furniture, and the Best Modes of Warming and Ventilating*. New York: D. Appleton & Company, 1852.

Dyson, Walter. 1921. *Howard University Studies in History*. Washington, DC: Howard University Press, 1921.

Henry, Christine Rae. "LeDroit Park, A Portrait in Black and White: A Study of Historic Districts, Social Change, and the Process of Neighborhood Placemaking." PhD thesis, University of Maryland, 2016.

Hightower, Barbara Elaine. "LeDroit Park: The Making of a Suburb, 1872–1888." Master's thesis, George Washington University, 1982.

Jackson, Lauretta. Oral history interview for the D.C. Humanities Council, November 21, 2009.

Johnson, Ronald M. "From Romantic Suburb to Racial Enclave: LeDroit Park, Washington, D.C., 1880–1920." *Phylon* 45, no. 4 (1984): 264–70.

Kennon, Donald R., and Richard Striner. 1983. *Washington Past and Present: A Guide to the Nation's Capital*. Washington, D.C.: United States Capitol Historical Society.

LeDroit Park Historic District Nomination, 1974. National Register of Historic Places Inventory—Nomination Form. https://planning.dc.gov.

Logan, Rayford W. *Howard University: The First Hundred Years 1867–1967*. New York: New York University Press, 1969.

McGill, James H. *James H. McGill's Architectural Advertiser*. Washington, DC: R. Reresford, printer, 1879.

Musgrove, George Derek, and Chris Myers Asch. *Chocolate City: A History of Race and Democracy in the Nation's Capital*. Chapel Hill: University of North Carolina Press, 2017.

A Plan for LeDroit Park. Washington, DC: D.C. Department of Housing & Community Development, 1979.

Report of the Commissioner of Indian Affairs for the Year 1865. Washington, DC: William A. Harris, 1865.

Roberts, Kim. *A Literary Guide to Washington, D.C.: Walking in the Footsteps of American Writers from Francis Scott Key to Zora Neale Hurston*. Charlottesville: University of Virginia Press, 2018.

"United States Census, 1880." Database with images, *FamilySearch*, Washington, District of Columbia, United States; citing enumeration district ED 4, sheet, NARA microfilm publication T9 (Washington, DC: National Archives and Records Administration, n.d.), FHL microfilm.

"United States Census, 1900." Database with images, *FamilySearch* NARA microfilm publication T623. Washington, D.C.: National Archives and Records Administration, n.d.

"United States Census, 1910." Database with images, *FamilySearch*, Precinct 8, Washington, District of Columbia, United States; citing enumeration district (ED) ED 159. NARA microfilm publication T624 (Washington, DC: National Archives and Records Administration, 1982), roll 153; FHL microfilm 1,374,166.

"United States Census, 1920." Database with images, *FamilySearch* Citing NARA microfilm publication T625. Washington, D.C.: National Archives and Records Administration, n.d.

"United States Census, 1930." Database with images, *FamilySearch*, Washington, District of Columbia, United States; citing enumeration district (ED) ED 227. NARA microfilm publication T626 (Washington, DC: National Archives and Records Administration, 2002), roll 298; FHL microfilm 2,340,033.

Washington at Home: An Illustrated History of Neighborhoods in the Nation's Capital. Baltimore, MD: Johns Hopkins University Press, 2010.

Washington on Foot, Fifth Edition: 24 Walking Tours and Maps of Washington, D.C., Old Town Alexandria, and Takoma Park. Washington, DC: Smithsonian, 2012.

Index

A

Adams, George W. 104
Albright, J. Joseph 117, 118
Archer, Louise 42
Archer, Romulus 42
Arlington National Cemetery 19,
      42, 91, 97, 99
Augusta, Dr. Alexander 19

B

Banes, Charles E. 26, 105, 126
Barber, Amzi L. 21, 52, 66, 103,
      117, 133, 134
Barnum, E.B. 58, 107
Benton, Frank 53
Birney, Arthur 60, 61
Birney, William 60, 61, 110
Brooke, Edward 118
Brown, Hilda Wilkinson 54, 149
Brown, Hiram and Susie 108, 141

Brown, Theresa 34, 116
Burdett, Samuel S. 97
Burrill, Mary P. 65
Butterworth, Benjamin 91

C

Campbell Hospital 16, 17, 19, 20,
      127
Campbell, Thomas B. 57
Carson, Simeon 48, 66
Choate, Warren 110
Cooper, Anna Julia 23, 52, 57, 71,
      74, 94, 111, 147

D

Darwin, Charles C. 80
Darwin, Gertrude Bascom 63
Deland, Eugenie 96
Deland, Theodore 96

De Priest, Jessie 108
De Priest, Oscar S. 108
Dudley, William W. 71
Dunbar, Alice 112, 113
Dunbar, Paul Laurence 112, 136, 139, 147

E

Eldridge, George D. 53, 58
Elks Lodge 50
Ellington, Duke 104, 119, 120, 141
Ethical Pharmacy 43
Evans, French S. 101
Evans, Lillian 85
Evermann, Barton W. 58

F

Fairman, Charles E. 114
First Separate Battalion 97, 99, 116
Fleetwood, Christian 94, 97, 115, 138, 139
Fleetwood, Sarah 115
Fletcher, Louis C. 72
Florida Avenue Baptist Church 41, 42
Ford, Ellery C. 94, 115
Frazier, Franklin 55
Frazier's Funeral Home 50
Freedmen's Hospital 19, 45, 48, 104
Frelinghuysen University 75, 94

G

Gage-Eckington Elementary School 125
Gannett, Henry 59, 63, 80
Gibbs, Harriet 123
Gibbs, Ida 74, 111, 123
Gilbert, Grove K. 92, 102
Gilman, Z.D. 14, 15, 16, 29, 31, 52, 133
Graydon, James W. 69
Griffith Stadium 54, 119, 120, 140, 141, 142, 144
Gurley Memorial Church 41, 42
Guyot, Lawrence 106

H

Hamilton, Julia West 87, 88, 94
Hamilton, West A. 87, 88, 99, 116
Harrison, Robert 47
Harrison's Cafe 47
Howardtown 19, 136
Howard University 133
Hughes, Langston 71, 136
Human Resources Development Group 45

I

Irish, Orasmus H. 62

J

Jackson, Algernon 56
Jackson, Lauretta 34, 117

Jamaica Vacancy 12, 21
Johnson, Arnold B. 94
Just, Ernest 88

K

Kendrick, Dolores 113, 114
Kennan, George 100
Kimball, Sumner I. 92

L

Lamasure, Edwin 102
Langdon, Andrew 21, 31, 52, 53,
    55, 117
Lawson, Rosetta 75, 94
Lincoln, Abraham 17, 46, 47
Locomobile 103, 118

M

Maddren, Joseph 126
Manna, Inc. 114
Manning, Van H. 72
Marvin, Joseph B. 99
McClelland, David 14, 15, 16, 21,
    24, 29, 31, 41, 50, 51, 133
McGill, James 23, 34, 117
Miller, May 33, 105, 119, 136
Moore, George 14, 16, 28, 133
M Street / Dunbar High School
    138
Mussey, Ellen 67
Mussey, Ruben D. 67

N

Nathanial Parker Gage School 128
Neal, Aline 45
Newman, Arthur 97, 99

O

Ohm, Frederick C. 121

P

Park at LeDroit 125, 126
Perry, Geneva 73
Peyton, Fountain 82
Prince, Howard L. 107

R

Rainbow Market 44
Richardson, Willis 105, 119, 136
Richards, William P. 125
Riggs, Harriet 109
Robinson, Hilyard 64, 127
Rose, Joseph N. 58
Ruoff, Charles 109

S

Slowe Hall 49, 64, 65, 127, 135
Smith, Josephine C. 128
Smith, W. Scott 101
Spencer, Lyman P. 69, 97
Syphax, Charles S. 88, 89, 97

T

Taliaferro, Clara Smyth 109, 141
Terrell, Mary Church 45, 52, 63, 74, 77, 82, 88, 94, 111, 123, 147
Terrell, Robert 42, 77, 79, 111, 135, 139
Terry, Lewis 43
Tibbs, Roy W. 85

W

Walker, Beatrice L. 99
Walker, James 97
Walker, John B. 103
Washington, Bennetta Bullock 86, 87
Washington, John E. 46
Washington, Walker 86, 87, 106, 135
Weatherless, Nelson 91
Whipper, Ionia 45
White, Charles A. 80, 92
Wilkinson, Garnet C. 110, 141
Williams, Octavius 113
Woog, Benjamin 83
Woog, Edmund 83, 85

Y

YWCA 92, 94, 111

About the Author

Canden Schwantes (now Arciniega) has been a historian and tour guide in Washington, D.C., for over a decade. She has published three other books about D.C. history, as well as numerous articles. She has been featured on the Travel Channel, the Discovery Channel, BBC, NPR and local news discussing D.C. history and tourism. Her company, Free Tours by Foot, operates worldwide, but her home and heart is in D.C. When she isn't writing about or leading tours of Washington, she is taking her two children on adventures in the city or supporting her husband, local musician Manny Arciniega, at his gigs.